The future of education

Letters to the Prime Minister

Edited by Ted Wragg

D1347978

The New Vision Group

Letters to the Prime Minister is
published by the New Vision Group.
The Group is a collection of
individuals who work in education
and are concerned for its future. It
began in 1993 and includes university
professors and others who work in
schools, colleges and local
government.

Copyright the New Vision Group

ISBN 0 9549972 0 4

Cover & design by Victoria McManus
Cover photos by Fred Jarvis
Printed by Amber Press

Acknowledgements

Although I have been the final editor of this collection of letters, I should like to thank all the contributors for their many attendances at discussions, and their promptness in writing their letters and responding to queries. I should like to thank also the people who made suggestions about content, though did not actually write a letter. Special thanks are due to Fred Jarvis who has acted as secretary to and convenor of the group, and who has done a considerable amount of work collecting and discussing the contributions.

Ted Wragg, Emeritus Professor of Education, Exeter University.

Contents

Contents

Contents

Letter 1

Introduction

Ted Wragg

Dear Prime Minister

So who are we, and why are we writing to you about education? The New Vision Group is a loose, in the nicest sense of the word, collection of people who work in education and are concerned about its future. In 1993, a number of us, mainly university professors in education, produced an alternative White Paper called Education: a Different Vision, published by the Institute for Public Policy Research. In it we argued against the style of public education we had at the time "which sees children as commodities, parents as consumers, schools as competitive businesses, teachers as technicians, the curriculum as a set of bureaucratic requirements, accountability as narrowly conceived test scores put into crude league tables, further and higher education as factories, power as something to be held and wielded by ministers, local democracy as an institution to be crushed, and pre-school, adult and community education as a luxury for the few, rather than the right of all".

Twelve years later, in 2005, an election year, the New Vision Group is amplified by a number of people from schools, colleges and local government. We meet from time to time to talk about the future of education, but we have no direct political power, nor are we, as a group, affiliated to any particular party. We do each possess a pen, however, so some of us are now taking the opportunity to write individual letters to you, the newly elected Prime Minister, expressing our hopes and fears for education in the 21st century.

Have things changed for the better in the last twelve years, and where should we be heading, half way through the first decade of the 21st century, if we are to have a truly 21st century form of education? In this collection of letters, we address the different ages and stages of education, from early years, through primary and secondary, the 14-19 phase, right up to further, higher and lifelong education. We also write about issues that straddle all types of education: access and opportunity, special educational needs, choice, assessment, finance, the local voice. All the writers are closely connected with the topic of the letter they have crafted and the great majority have also carried out years of intensive research in the field, so they write not just with enthusiasm and commitment, but with authority. As they are writing a letter, the authors have not included references to the research and evidence they cite, but these are available from them should they be needed.

A personal view

Although I am acting as editor, as I did in the 1993 Education: a Different Vision papers, I also want to express some personal views that may or may not be shared by other contributors. Much of what has happened in education during the last few years has been positive, some of it has been neutral, other aspects have been poor, in certain cases a cause for alarm.

The good things must survive. I hope the high profile that education has enjoyed in recent times will be sustained. The analysis I have done of the annual British Attitudes Survey over the last twenty years shows that education is seen by people as coming second to health in importance, year after year, but the public now rate it closer to health than it used to be. In the 21st century, when highly interactive technologies offer access to some of the greatest repositories of knowledge and multimedia libraries in the world, a high quality structure for education is still vital - through the First Age, the period of full-time education and training; the Second Age, the phase of work; and the Third Age, the time of healthy retirement.

There are other good features to preserve. Programmes like Sure Start for the early years, Education Action Zones, and Excellence in Cities (don't forget rural areas, for they can suffer from deprivation as well) have been welcomed in schools. So have wider social policies over which schools have no direct control, but which can have an impact on what they are trying to achieve, such as neighbourhood regeneration schemes and taking families, especially those with children, out of poverty. More money for books and equipment, better financial rewards for teachers (though greater sources of aggravation), an updating programme that will see every one of the five secondary schools and several primary schools in Exeter, the city where I live, replaced by a brand new building, all these are positive. So is the new children's agenda, Every Child Matters, which is beginning to succeed in bringing all the services that deal with children closer together, long overdue.

There are, unfortunately, a number of much more negative features. Many relate to the excessive accountability agenda that sees teachers spending too much time ticking boxes and filling in forms, cutting back severely on the time and energy available for their teaching. Reception class teachers have to tick 117 different boxes to profile their five year olds. Utterly ludicrous. Good management secures accountability, but minimises bureaucracy in order to maximise the time people spend on the ball, doing the job for which they are paid, not just

11

accounting for it. It is like a football team coming off half way through the first half to plan the second. When they return they are 25-0 down.

Teachers are not alone. Consultants complain they spend five hours a week more than they used to on bureaucracy; police officers take minutes to make an arrest, but hours to write it up. Still, the government did try. Two committees were set up to look into the problems of duplication, but neither knew the other existed. Early in the morning I write satirical newspaper articles and comedy scripts for Rory Bremner. Alas, satire will soon be declared officially dead, for it can no longer compete with real life.

Another problem is the plethora of political initiatives that a number of writers refer to in these letters. Some initiatives are fine, but the 'wheeze a week' approach has been in mode since Kenneth Baker was Secretary of State in the late 1980s. No sooner have some initiatives been born than they are suffocated – beacon schools, Education Action Zones, Best Practice Research Fellowships for teachers. They come, they go, like ships in the night. A toot on the foghorn and yet another one comes along, solely to prevent the public thinking the government has run out of steam.

One suggestion, Prime Minister: put more effort into making the best initiatives work and end the culture of useless idea generation that emanates from your own office. When the AS and A level mayhem was at its height, with some pupils taking five exams in a single day, and even having to stay overnight at a teacher's home if a paper had to be held over, what was the Number 10 Unit doing? Sorting out the mess? Quite the reverse. It was proposing a third A level, the Advanced Extension exam. Had this taken off, the whole system would have collapsed. It is a crazy way to run education.

That leads to one of my most important points. The Prime Minister's own office has now accrued phenomenal power and control, a thoroughly unhealthy state of affairs in a British-style democracy. When I interviewed James Callaghan for Radio 4 in 1986, on the tenth anniversary of his Ruskin College speech, he said that it was for the Prime Minister to start a debate, but for ministers to see it through.

The dramatic change in political climate began with Margaret Thatcher. In an amazing parallel to more recent events, the Higginson committee, chaired by a vice chancellor in 1987/88, proposed a five subject slate instead of A levels. There was broad agreement about what was suggested, but the Prime Minister turned it down, on the grounds that A levels must not be touched.

From 2003 to 2005 former chief inspector of schools, Mike Tomlinson, carried out a similar enquiry, again securing a high degree of agreement across education and business. Once more it was the Prime Minister who shovelled it under the carpet, in a panic over right-wing press reaction to the reform of A levels, despite the report being endorsed by such distinguished institutions as Cambridge University, hardly intellectual vandals. A golden opportunity to introduce a set of curriculum and assessment options that could appeal to young people of different abilities was spurned, simply on the say so of the Prime Minister. This tight central control and the crude isosceles triangle of command, with one person at the top, is an especially chilling feature of education today. It is in your hands to do something about it. Effective leadership is not synonymous with dictatorship.

This illustrates the nub of the problem. Some adolescents, lacking the structure and support of a stable home, seeing themselves, and being seen, as failures in a system driven by examination success, turn to antisocial behaviour inside and outside school. The answer lies partly in engaging them in an exacting curriculum that is more appropriate than what they are currently offered. The Tomlinson report tried to set this in motion, without diluting

13

what was on offer to the more orthodox, but such is the power of the Prime Minister today, that two years of work, and extensive consultation, costing a huge amount of money and time, were overturned at a stroke. What is the point? Why bother 'consulting' at all? It would be better to listen to those who know much more about children and schools than pale-faced policy wonks, and to those who practise the art and science of teaching.

Sometimes good ideas are emasculated by the insertion of one or two especially daft elements. The Work Force remodelling exercise is one such example. In itself it is an excellent notion – to use teachers' skills more effectively. But the whole initiative is spoiled by insisting that unqualified classroom assistants should teach classes on their own, and also by not funding it promptly and sufficiently. Good idea, lousy delivery.

I offer the following seven (therefore lucky) point plan, that you as the new Prime Minister could implement without any great ceremony, given your immense potency. It is not meant to be comprehensive (ooops, wash my mouth out with soap and water), just mentioning a few points that might help.

Set schools free, I mean really free, from the suffocating central control set up by your predecessors. They can still be accountable. According to the 2002 Education Act, schools have to apply in writing to the minister to innovate. They even have to fill in a ludicrous form, which among other delectables, asks for an 'exit strategy' - what they will do to return to their previous practice, once their licence to innovate has expired. Imagine Dr Christian Barnard's surgical innovation licence running out, so he has to rush round all his transplant patients reinserting their old hearts (good job he had kept them in the fridge). Dear minister, please may I innovate? What an insult.

Scrap the 117 tickboxes for five year olds, over 3,500 for a class. Let the poor beggars have a childhood and allow reception class teachers to down their clipboards and go back to teaching them.

Set up a proper curriculum for 14 to 19 year olds. If not the Tomlinson proposals, then at least something that does not look backwards to programmes that are of no interest to a sizeable, and worrying minority. A better curriculum, accompanied by effective teaching, would do more for discipline than a hundred strongarm initiatives.

Wield a giant flame thrower on the 30,000,000 exam papers (a fifteen-fold increase in recent years) taken each summer and turned round within a few weeks; their dominance is out of all proportion to their yield.

Pursue a policy of fairness for all, not elitism. City academies costing millions can easily become selective (as research into American magnet schools has shown) and drain the schools round about of talent and social muscle. Differentiated top-up fees for universities, and they will no doubt come, favour the better off, who can better contemplate £10,000 to £15,000 a year for elite institutions, while the poor blanche at the thought. Segregated 1st, 2nd and 3rd class Victorian railway carriages are the wrong model for 21st century education. Let us have more of what the city Exeter is doing – all five high schools with brand new buildings, not one gold-plated palace and four clapped out dumps.

Introduce an inspection system that works. OFSTED has been a 'how not to' model – mechanical, formulaic, repressive, inimical to innovation (many teachers are terrified to innovate in case OFSTED calls). It was no surprise when a retired army general, who had become chairman of his local primary school governing body, wrote to the Times castigating OFSTED as a waste of time and money, certainly not what they would do in the army, where the emphasis would be on putting right what is going wrong. Local and national inspectors should work more closely together, with the former following up inspections in an advisory way to see what is happening.

Improve relationships with the teaching profession. Successive governments have rubbished teachers, with considerable negative effects on morale. Some politicians believe that bashing teachers wins votes. I am not even sure of that. Most teachers want to work in partnership, rather than in conflict, with the government, but not if the message is "Join our crusade, you clueless amateurs".

Finally, Prime Minister, please pound the Number 10 Policy Unit into a very small ploughshare. Untold bounties will accrue.

Yours sincerely

Ted Wragg

Ted Wragg is Emeritus Professor of Education at Exeter University

Letter 2

Tackling disadvantage, disaffection and underachievement

Tim Brighouse

Dear Prime Minister,

Her Majesty's Chief Inspector reported in 2003 that there are 10,000 teenagers not in secondary school. There are many more than this number physically attending but who are not sharing in the schools' collective and dramatic improvement in performance. Indeed these youngsters at 16 - usually called NEET (not in employment, education and training) are settling for far less than they have the potential to achieve in their early teenage years. They are often resigned to the inevitability of an unfulfilling and comparatively short life spent at best on the margins of society, at worst in antisocial and sometimes criminal activity at great cost to themselves and others. It is on their behalf that I write this letter.

One of the driving purposes of any caring government should be to even up life's chances so that those born in challenging circumstances have a better chance of fulfilling their potential to their own and other's advantage. Cracking the cycle of disadvantage, or eradicating the worst generational effects of poverty is how some describe it.

It's to the credit of the present government that they set in train so many general and specific measures especially in education to tackle the issue. In the period 1997 to 2000 the Social Inclusion Unit provided nearly two dozen reports all personally endorsed by the Prime Minister, which illustrated vividly and comprehensively what is needed to help overcome the greatest inequalities suffered by those in the margins of our society.

Many initiatives introduced between 1997 and 2005 have contributed to this end. For example, history will pick out the ambitious, well funded reforms and expanded provision for the Early Years. Now there is a ready availability of part and full time nursery provision and of wrap-around care in pre school settings whether in nursery schools and classes, Sure Start or Neighbourhood Nurseries. This will change for the better the experience in the most formative years for the children of the most challenged families. The connected reforms to the benefit and tax system will also help our poorest children. At the other end of the statutory period of education the introduction of maintenance allowances for 16 – 19 year olds, coupled with grants and top-up fees and changes in access to university, means that when these young people from poorer families grow up they will be more likely to take full advantage of higher education and well rewarded career opportunities.

It is, however, in the period in between – the school years – that the new government needs more boldly to refine and extend what's been attempted in the period 1997 – 2005. Of course many general and specific initiatives in this period have all made a difference. The Literacy and Numeracy Strategies, the Key Stage 3 strategy and targeted standard funds (for example pupil credits, social exclusion and study support) have helped. Even the reform of the Careers Service through Connexions was spoilt only by the poor management of a good idea. Moreover the "Excellence in Cities" (EiC) programme in particular has provided welcome necessary and extra support (almost 5% on average per school) and focus (for example learning mentors and enrichment experiences for the gifted and talented) to urban secondary schools. This focus acknowledges implicitly that 85% of our most disadvantaged pupils are in urban schools.

Indeed EiC must have had some causal impact on the accelerating progress – much faster than in more affluent areas – of urban schools' achievements. I know in depth and from first hand experience the extraordinary transformation of expectation, skill and outcome in schools in Birmingham and London. The improvement in these two cities is dramatic and the average five or more higher grade GCSE percentages are now at or above the national average where fifteen years ago they were half that figure. In which other country does the first and second city perform at levels like this?

Nevertheless we expect and need much more. The by-product of so many more youngsters achieving five or more higher grades at GCSE has been to throw into sharp relief the gap between them and 20 – 30% of youngsters who are themselves increasingly aware of their comparative failure. They are disillusioned with their prospects and increasingly alienated. These youngsters are over represented in figures for school exclusions – especially fixed term exclusions – truancy, drug abuse, youth crime and eventually homelessness. They often come from poor and challenging background, where parents and carers find it a formidable challenge to provide good enough support.

In short these statistics show a close correlation if no necessary causality. So the comparative lack of achievement of black - especially youngsters from Caribbean extraction – mixed race and white working class youngsters - especially boys - continue to be a running sore in our system. Some schools have given focused attention to some of those comparatively disadvantaged groups. As you know, all schools now have the data and skills of analysis to do this. Nevertheless they are operating within a system which doesn't overtly reward them for their efforts. Even the recently introduced value added tables mean that to receive a Year 7 pupil with a Level 5 and then convert it to a series of A* GCSE grades in Year 11 will count as much, or more, as overcoming the formidable barriers experienced by a Level 3 boy in achieving a GCSE Level C five years later. The second task is incomparably harder, requires more skill, determination and resolve on the part of teacher and learner alike and is more likely to address the needs of the socially excluded. Performance targets like this need to be changed to encourage the focus which will overcome social exclusion.

So if we can take as a priority for your government the reduction of the underachievement of large numbers of socially challenged youngsters, what needs to be done? I suggest some changes to the funding, regulation, inspection and accountability processes – systemic changes without which the best efforts of staff in schools will continue to be undermined.

First, funding: one of the first tasks for your new Secretary of State will be to propose for 2006/7 new and simplified arrangements for the formula by which schools receive their delegated budgets. One of the unfortunate features of the first introduction of Local Management of Schools (LMS) was the very low percentage – between 1% and 8% of the total funds – for Additional Educational Needs (AEN) or the proportion to allow for disadvantage. This low percentage has persisted in subsequent changes to the process. Almost all LEAs have used eligibility for free school meals as the main criterion for distributing this element of the budget. Recent governments have supplemented this sum through Excellence in Cities and various standards funds. In simplifying and reforming the funding system for 2006 it would be possible to introduce for secondary schools – a similar scheme based on externally validated Base Line assessments on entry could be introduced for Primary Schools – a flat rate £2,500 per capita entitlement for youngsters entering with Level 3, £3,500 for Level 2 and £4,500 for less than Level 2.

If this per annum addition were linked to value added at Key Stage 3 and 4 performance – judged by suitable criteria across the whole achievement, attendance and behaviour range - then schools would have incentives to concentrate their efforts on those who need most help, as well as those who are going to deliver headline scores in terms of five or more higher grade GCSEs. £500 of each of these sums could be in the form of a voucher to be spent by parents on approved extra educational provision made by a group of schools beyond the normal school day, week and year.

There are two reasons for this. I say "group of schools" because no school alone can meet all the needs of all their pupils. (In an age of zero tolerance and league tables, there is considerable temptation for the individual school, either directly or indirectly, to exclude pupils, or not to admit them in the first place). Pinning the responsibility on groups (collegiates, or federations) of co-operating schools seems the best way of minimising this practice. Secondly the involvement of the hardest to reach parents and carers in the form of an "education extra" voucher would surely help to support the aims of the school and society as a whole not to allow the cycle of deprivation to repeat itself.

A further reform of funding would also help. Schools – and often their most challenged pupils – have benefited from summer schools, weekend courses and after-hours learning funded by standards funds, New Opportunities Funding (now the Big Lottery) and other bespoke funds such as Neighbourhood Renewal. These funds have no long term guarantees. It is time to consolidate them into a national scheme for "Third Session" funding, with a combination of national and local taxation targeted to need as defined by socio-economic disadvantage. Such funding would finance all sorts of different provision including those made by the voluntary sector, the much under valued Youth Service (which does so much for the most challenged youngsters) as well as groups of schools.

For these changes in funding to achieve sustained changes of habit and focus within schools, requires complementary changes in inspection and measures of accountability. Through annual published results and inspections, schools should identify say two chronically underachieving groups and show what progress they are making against their previous best and comparatively as a result of the school's programme of interventions. The key question is: "Are such youngsters being swept along – rather then swept aside – by the school's ever stronger achievement culture?" The performance of groups of co-operating schools needs to be inspected by OFSTED as well as the individual school. For in this system the group will be achieving on inclusion, which the individual school cannot.

If these simple changes along with the recommendations for the curriculum and school admissions made by other correspondents are made by you and your Secretary of State, an already improving schooling system would be seen as the world leader it can so easily be.

Yours sincerely,

Tim Brighouse

Tim Brighouse is Senior Adviser, London Schools, and Visiting Professor, Institute of Education, London University

The early years
Bob Janes

Dear Prime Minister,

The lives of children and families throughout the country have been radically changed over the last few years as the introduction of free nursery education and the development of childcare has impacted on all communities.

In 1997 the provision of both Early Years Education and Childcare was spread very unevenly across the country. In 2005 early years education and childcare are central to the policy of all political parties. The progress achieved in this sector has been nothing short of astounding with clear success in delivery of services and sustained enthusiasm for continuous development and improvement. The Labour Government set an ambitious long term objective to end child poverty by 2020 and has introduced the Children Act, focusing on outcomes for children and young people based on consultation with them about what they consider to be important in improving their lives. These 5 outcomes of being healthy, staying safe, economic wellbeing, achieving and enjoying and contributing and participation form the basis on which children's services for the future will be judged.

Since 1998 over a million new childcare places have been created and there is now an entitlement of free nursery education for all 3 and 4 year olds.

Approximately 30% of the youngest children in the most disadvantaged communities are benefiting from additional services through Sure Start local programmes. In addition to ending child poverty, policy developments have been aimed at creating opportunities for flexible working and are now moving towards providing parenting support for every parent who wants it and early identification of children at risk, in order to give them the support that they need. So it is from a strong base that future developments may occur.

The ultimate aim of the next government should be a free childcare place for all children up to the age of 14, with direct grants to providers being the primary funding mechanism. It is suggested that this free entitlement would include 3 afternoons per week out of school care and 5 weeks per year holiday care, which at current rates amounts to approximately £1500 per child per year. (Price Waterhouse Cooper have recently done some research to cost the benefits of a childcare entitlement for the UK). In recognition that a free childcare place for all may not be immediately within grasp the following groups of children should be considered for priority:

- Children looked after
- 'Children in need' (DoH)
- Young carers and their siblings
- Children with additional needs
- Carers returning to work for the first month
- Childcare for carers attending training leading to employment

Childcare for Children Looked After has the benefit of stability of placements and better outcomes for the children and young people. It also helps to recruit and retain foster carers. However, foster carers are not able to claim Working Families Tax Credit because they receive a small amount of monetary support from the Local Authority. But the funding available to foster carers from the Local Authority is not considered generous enough to pay for childcare for the children concerned.

There are two possible ways in which the childcare entitlement could be implemented across the country for all looked after children:

- Ringfenced funding being allocated to Social Services for childcare provision according to identified need, i.e. numbers of children looked after in the authority.

- Including foster carers in the cohort of carers able to claim Working Families Tax Credit and ringfencing a smaller amount of money to Social Services, so that they could afford the additional amount of money that foster carers would need to pay for the childcare entitlement.

Since 1998 there has been a greater emphasis on training for childcare workers. If standards in the childcare sector are to continuously improve then this emphasis needs to remain and be developed further. Early years education and childcare workers should be a well qualified and salaried workforce. In order the achieve this, the following may be considered:

- Regarding foster carers and residential workers as childcarers and therefore affording them the same opportunities and responsibilities to attend regular training, leading to nationally recognised qualification courses, as other childcare workers.

- Introducing 5 in-service training days, that are nationally agreed, for all workers within children's services to attend training and professional development opportunities, much of which should be multi-agency. There also needs to be a nationally agreed objective that, for example 60% should have a graduate level qualification by 2015, with the other 40% having Level 3 qualifications by that date.

Developments have included a move towards increased participation and contribution from children and young people themselves. For the first time, children and young people have been instrumental in shaping national legislation in defining the 5 outcomes in the Children Act. However, in order to continue to shape services that best meet the needs of children and young people they need to be fully involved. Developments in this area may include:

- Introducing a standard within all inspections of children's services relating to contribution and participation and ensuring that all children's services can show evidence of how carers, children and young people have been involved in the planning, delivery and review of services.

- A national peer mentoring scheme should be considered, which would provide universal and targeted support to children and young people, particularly at points of transition, and would contribute to the 'Staying Safe' agenda and meet the needs of children with low levels of difficulties.

- Consideration may be given to introducing a school organised national community service requirement of 2 hours a week for all young people in year 12. This would change society's perception of young people and may be based on the interests of young people themselves, for example involving them in maintenance of their local parks, in coaching the children's football team, in accompanying disabled young children on swimming sessions etc.

- Children and young people need more encouragement to engage in constructive leisure pursuits, including opportunity to participate in music, arts and sports activity at little or no cost.

Children's services are not just about children, they are about the support that parents and families have in bringing up those children. Early intervention/ Preventative services need to be strengthened in order to increase the impact on the lives of some of the most vulnerable young children. Sure Start Local Programmes and Children's Fund Services are beginning to show how effective services can be in meeting the needs of local communities. There has been a substantial level of funding to support these developments, but the real change has occurred as a result of refocusing services in response to needs identified by the local families.

Research indicates 6 areas of early intervention/preventative services that are particularly beneficial to children and families. These are as follows:

- Early family support
- Mediation service for families in conflict
- Counselling for both children and adults suffering domestic violence situations
- Personal signposting services
- Services for both children and families in situations where there are issues of drug and alcohol abuse
- Benefits/welfare advice

These services need to be provided in a non-stigmatised environment through non-statutory providers wherever possible.

Parent and toddler groups are effective as low level family support. Local authorities could have a duty to be pro-active in planning the development and maintenance of parent and toddler groups to a recognised quality assurance system. In addition to meeting low level needs they are often the starting point for parent and carers who may wish to return to work.

As support grows for children, young people and their families, information regarding their entitlements to services should be widely available.

Parents could be issued with a card detailing the entitlement of provision for their children, including library membership, free early years education, access to childcare and so on. This could be sponsored by retailers who could offer discounts to parents and carers in purchasing goods for children and young people.

At present local service directories are not co-ordinated or linked making it difficult for children, families and professionals to find information. Consideration should be given to developing a national single data source for services for children and families, building on the SureStartChildcarelink childcare website.

In conclusion:

Since 1997 there has been a fundamental change in the way society thinks about services for children, young people and families. The emphasis now is on services being designed and delivered to meet the needs of the children, ensuring that they have the best possible opportunity to realise their full potential.

The early years and childcare agenda is central to tackling child poverty and improving lives of children and families. The challenge now is to build on the excellent work that has already achieved real change within society, and to ensure that the voices of children, young people and families are heard at every stage of the process. As Professor A. Aynsley-Green (National Clinical Director for Children) says, "children and young people are important. They are the living message we send to a time we will not see. Nothing matters more to families than the health, welfare and future success of their children. They deserve the best care because they are the life blood of the nation and are vital for the future economic survival and prosperity".

The practical challenge is how to ensure that children's services locally are coherent in design and delivery with good coordination, effective joint working between and across sectors and agencies, with smooth transitions and in partnership with children, young people and families.

Yours Sincerely,

Bob Janes

Bob Janes is Chair of Derbyshire Early Years Partnership

Letter 4

The Primary Curriculum:
An overdue case for reform

Robin Alexander

Dear Prime Minister,

First, let us be thankful that primary education is no longer the Cinderella of public education, confined to the servants' hall of policy, while secondary and higher education pirouette and hobnob in the ballroom. The belief that educating children aged 5-11 is a sideshow, and that teaching them is in every sense child's play, has at last begun to yield to a simple, demonstrable and indeed momentous truth: that humans learn more and faster during their pre-adolescent years than at any other stage of their lives, and that what and how they are taught during those years profoundly conditions their future prospects and hence their contribution to the society in which they grow up. Primary education is a matter of the utmost importance.

Politicians of all parties can take some credit for attending to this belated cultural shift. But they must also acknowledge that it wouldn't have happened without the sustained advocacy of those teachers, academics, inspectors and parents who have argued the case for primary education in the teeth of well over a century of patronising disdain from governments no less than from the educational establishment.

Such benighted attitudes, though, haven't entirely

disappeared. The Janet and John tone of much that DfES sends out to primary schools attests to that. Do those who write this stuff really think that people who teach small children have small minds? Do officials or advisers whose ignorance of learning and teaching is matched only by their callow arrogance really believe that they have a right to tell primary teachers what to do and how to think? Would they try this on with any other professional group?

It would be a mistake, too, to conclude from the initiative deluge of the past few years that primary education is now, as they say, 'sorted'. The picture remains decidedly mixed. Not all the recent initiatives have been properly researched and conceived, let alone successful. The quality of provision is uneven. Some of the most fundamental needs of a modern system of primary education haven't even been accepted as such, let alone addressed.

Take the curriculum. In 1988 the Conservatives introduced a national curriculum, thus at last giving all primary pupils an entitlement to a reasonably broad foundation of knowledge, understanding and skill. That was an important gain. But they did so with such disregard for the logistics of the whole that it rapidly proved unmanageable. And properly concerned about standards though the Conservatives were, they also imposed the whole debatable apparatus of national tests and league tables in a way which turned many primary schools into OFSTED-fearing SAT crammers.

The Conservatives also initiated projects to tackle the undeniably serious problem of poor and patchy standards in literacy and numeracy. Again, a positive development with not wholly positive consequences. New Labour stepped in and repackaged these two projects as multi-million pound national literacy and numeracy strategies with targets, deadlines, support materials and a tightly-specified approach to planning and teaching which all schools were invited (for the strategies were technically non-statutory), but in effect obliged to adopt.

The government then intervened, twice, and very damagingly, in the process of primary curriculum reform. First it instructed the Qualifications and Curriculum Authority (QCA), the body responsible for the scheduled 1997-8 National Curriculum review, not to ask, as any review worth its name should, whether the KS1/2 curriculum was right for today's children and tomorrow's society, but instead to tidy it up at the margins, and change as little as possible so that teachers could concentrate all their attention on the daily Literacy Hour and Numeracy Lesson. Second, for a hapless generation of children the 1988 principle of curriculum entitlement was sacrificed on the altar of 'standards', when in 1998 ministers decreed that primary schools need do no more than 'have regard to' the programmes of study for the seven non-core subjects. I was a member of the Board of QCA at the time: I remember these episodes, and our frustration at ministers' imperviousness to both reason and evidence, only too well.

What happened? In many primary schools, as OFSTED later revealed, the curriculum beyond the protected zone of literacy and numeracy was squeezed almost out of existence or was simply abandoned. Was this necessary? OFSTED reports from 1997 and 2002 showed that it was not, for the schools which did best in literacy and numeracy also most successfully sustained curriculum breadth and balance, while those that did worst failed to do so. It's obvious, really: you can't teach the basics in a vacuum. Curriculum breadth is about standards no less than entitlement. The evidence was there, but ministers ignored it. Not for the first time, or the last.

So we come up to date, with a Primary National Strategy which claims to usher in an era of breadth, balance, enrichment and creativity for children in our primary schools. Do not be deceived: by this grand gesture government is merely giving back in 2005 what it took away in 1998. If it is doing even that: with at least fifty per cent of the week mandatorily devoted to Literacy Hours and Numeracy Lessons, the problem of curriculum manageability stands exactly as it did in the early 1990s. Meanwhile, beyond the see-saw of hastily-cobbled policy, the big questions about the proper goals and character of a primary curriculum for the 21st century remain unasked and so unanswered.

What about the implications of the recent tendency towards political intervention in the way the curriculum is, in DfES and Postman Pat parlance, 'delivered'? Does that, too, give pause for thought? Well, it's self-evident that how schools teach is as important as what they teach and that curriculum acquires meaning for children only as classroom transactions. Yet even in the most centralised national education systems, governments have been wary about translating that truism into prescription.

Thus, in 1992, though he had clear views on the matter, the then Secretary of State prefaced the so-called 'three wise men' report on primary education (of which I was co-author) by insisting that 'questions about how to teach are not for Government to determine'. From 1998 such restraint was cast aside and a regime of four-part literacy lessons, three-part numeracy lessons, interactive whole class teaching, plenaries and all the rest was imposed on every primary school in England.

Of course, had the impact of all this on standards been decisive and unequivocal, such unprecedented interference in a profession's day-to-day decisions and practices might just have been excusable. But the evidence offers no such comfort, though you wouldn't think so from the triumphant spin from the Downing Street Delivery Unit.

Thus, while overall the KS2 test results from 1997 onwards may seem encouraging, the long tail of underachievement which distinguishes England's scholastic performance from that of many other countries stubbornly persists. Then, far from endorsing the literacy and numeracy strategies, the government's own evaluation (by the University of Toronto) reported that 'it is difficult to draw conclusions about the effect of the Strategies on pupil learning', while evidence from the many independent research studies has proved even less decisive. A major longitudinal study of primary numeracy standards from 1997-2002 concluded that the numeracy strategy 'had a positive but small effect on numeracy standards' but that 'there are many schools, children and areas of mathematics for whom the effect has been negligible or negative.'

Several other studies have tracked the impact of so-called 'interactive whole class teaching' in the light of the weighty psychological and neuroscientific evidence about the crucial role of high-quality talk on children's thinking and understanding in the early and primary years. They conclude that far from stretching young children's minds, the literacy and numeracy strategies have promoted classroom interaction which all too often is low-level and cognitively undemanding. And an exhaustive round-up of no fewer than eleven separate national and international studies of primary pupils' achievement, including of course the KS2 tests, has judged that there are far too many data anomalies, statistically faulty procedures and test protocol changes for the government's claims about rising standards to be sustained with anything like the confidence which is needed if such results are reliably to inform or legitimate policy.

But instead of the debate which should have attended these disturbing findings all we heard from government was 'the best standards ever', endlessly repeated, and this takes me from the primary curriculum and attendant questions about teaching, learning and standards to the way these are handled.

It's depressingly axiomatic that governments tend to devise policies and then look for evidence to support them. The National Literacy Strategy is a striking example:

someone was actually commissioned to find evidence to sustain this initiative after it had been signed, sealed, delivered and introduced to schools. 'Evidence-based policy' is the mantra: 'policy-based evidence' might be more apt.

But beware the policy boomerang. If from 1997 to 2004 government had been more responsive to evidence about the relationship between curriculum breadth and standards - a relationship which to most people is plain common sense but to the government's standards boffins seems to have been counter-intuitive – then standards would actually have benefited and the education of the primary class of 1997 wouldn't have been so impoverished.

The same goes for the examples I have just given from research on the impact of the national literacy and numeracy strategies. To such evidence - rigorously collected and analysed, validated by peer scrutiny – the Department's response is instinctively dismissive and indeed defensive. In the Primary Strategy manifesto Excellence and Enjoyment the bending and selective use of evidence is nothing short of breathtaking. We - the country, the education system, our children - simply can't afford such small-minded shuffling in the corridors of power.

And what of the vision? Celebrating the current nostrums of personalisation and choice, DfES tells us that by age 14 pupils will be in a position to choose those subjects and pathways which they find most relevant and worthwhile. But offering choice to pupils at age 14 demands that education at Key Stages 1 and 2, not just at Key Stage 3, should provide a foundation of sufficient breadth, depth and consistency to make that choice meaningful. Alas, we are nowhere near that point, thanks in part to recent policy.

Choice as envisaged also requires that the curriculum up to age 14 is demonstrably right for our changing world, for choice needs purpose and vision as well as a foundation. That's problematic too, thanks again to the refusal of successive governments to countenance genuinely open and radical thinking about the goals and content of public primary education. Instead we have an updated version of the Victorian elementary school curriculum: the 3Rs, a nod in the direction of the arts and humanities but only when it doesn't impede the current policy wheeze, and lots more simply bolted on as it comes into vogue – ICT, citizenship, PSHE, MFL and so on.

Is it right that primary school 'standards' should still be defined exclusively in terms of reading, writing and number, crucial though these are? Is it right that all other forms of human understanding, enquiry and endeavour should at the primary stage be relegated to mere 'enrichment', and then denied the time to make that label even half-way convincing? What, really, should 21st century educational 'basics' entail? Where, again, is the debate?

For there's the rub. In under two decades England has acquired one of the most centralised education systems going. True, much has been delegated to schools, but over that which government believes matters most - the curriculum, assessment, teaching methods, teacher training, quality assurance (the real core of education, in other words) - control from Sanctuary Buildings and Downing Street is now absolute.

Many of us would like to see that control relaxed, in the interests of education, quality and – yes – standards. Please abandon, too, both the patronising retold-for-little-teachers tone of what DfES sends to primary schools and the macho gobbledegook of 'tough', 'new', 'hard-hitting', 'step change', 'delivery', 'driving up', 'leading edge', 'world class', 'one-stop shop', 'best practice' and so on with which policy is invariably spun.

Educational 'best practice', incidentally, is the outcome not of political compliance but of enquiry, evidence, a lively debate about values and - something only the teacher can achieve - the judicious matching of decision to circumstance. One size, as government itself has told us, doesn't fit all. If we are to devise a primary curriculum which truly provides an educational foundation for choice, employment, active citizenship and the good society, and which equips children for the difficult and perhaps decisive decades ahead, we'll need a lot more humility, honesty and rigour at the top. That and a proper respect for language.

Yours Sincerely,

Robin Alexander

Robin Alexander is a Fellow of Wolfson College, University of Cambridge, and Emeritus Professor of Education, University of Warwick

Letter 5
Developing comprehensive education
Geoff Whitty

Dear Prime Minister

We have moved in our lifetime from an education system that failed the majority of young people to one in which there have been year on year increases in success rates. It is easy now to forget the huge wastage of talent that was associated with the old tripartite system of education. There is little doubt that the ending of academic selection at 11+ and the introduction of comprehensive secondary education has allowed many more people to succeed at school and go on to further and higher education, yet politicians and the press too often present it as a reform that has failed.

Indeed, there are even rumours in the papers that both major parties will seek to reintroduce academic selection after the election. This would be a retrograde step. It would be much better to end what 11+ selection remains and help complete the comprehensive transformation of Britain.

Academic performance

The best evidence suggests that most children benefit academically in comprehensive schools. When you consider that many so-called comprehensive schools have an ability range more like that of secondary modern schools, this performance is a remarkable testament to their academic success.

It is true that some research has shown that, at the highest academic levels, comprehensive school pupils currently do slightly less well than their peers in state grammar schools and academically selective private schools. However, what is remarkable is how small that difference is when selective schools have much narrower intakes, better qualified teachers and better facilities.

If the most able children in comprehensive schools can perform almost as well as - and in some cases outperform - those in schools which have a mission that is geared directly to their needs and not much else, then comprehensive schools can hardly be regarded as failures.

So, even in terms of the academic criteria that inform so much of the debate about the success or failure of comprehensive schools, they have not done at all badly. When we add to the equation the important fact that comprehensive schools contribute greatly to the inclusion agenda as well the standards agenda, it is particularly puzzling that they are not congratulated for their achievements.

Specialisation without selection

Recent governments have preferred to celebrate diversity as an alternative to comprehensive education - but it doesn't have to be. Advocates of comprehensive education have never denied the importance of diversity – it was not we who coined the term 'bogstandard'! Indeed, those of us who have worked in comprehensive schools know that each such school has its own ethos.

So you really don't need to present specialist schools as somehow other than comprehensive. You may be surprised to know that the great pioneer of comprehensive education, Caroline Benn, wrote many years ago that, "if schools merely make a particular activity their speciality, but keep their entry itself non-selective, they are comprehensive schools with a special facility or activity". Some of the very best of today's specialist schools are comprehensive schools in this sense, so now that 60% of secondary schools have a specialism, why not make sure they are all academically and socially comprehensive as well?

Those specialist schools that achieve their excellent results with balanced intakes should be seen as part of the success story of comprehensive education, so why not say unequivocally, as Estelle Morris once did, that specialist schools are "only modern comprehensive schools"? If selection is not a necessary condition for their success – and, in most cases, it appears not to be – we hope you will now confront the problem of those schools that do try to gain unfair advantage over others by covert selection.

A key issue for a comprehensive future – certainly in London and other big cities – is thus admissions policy. It is clear that social and academic polarisation between schools increases with the proportion of schools controlling their own admission policies. Common admissions policies and more adequate monitoring are essential if abuse is to be prevented. This is not incompatible with parental choice, but it is to make choice fairer and genuinely open to all. As Caroline Benn put it, "the sooner selection masquerading as specialisation ends, the sooner genuine diversity and alternative approaches can flourish".

Within a diverse system, the aim must be to find ways of preventing legitimate differences becoming unjustifiable inequalities and to stop particular social groups monopolising particular sorts of schools. There are many examples of equitable choice policies working successfully elsewhere in the world.

Pursuing inclusion

Inclusion, as part of the comprehensive vision, should not be seen as just a matter of engaging disadvantaged groups, vital as that is for a just society. Inclusive comprehensive schools need to embrace both middle and working class pupils, wherever this is geographically feasible. A school cannot be considered truly comprehensive if particular social groups are effectively excluded from its benefits, either by choice or by default.

For comprehensive education to move forward, it is vital to ensure that the middle classes see mainstream public education as the right place for their children rather than opt out into their own schools, whether public or private. School choice policies have sometimes facilitated a strategic withdrawal of the middle classes, making it even more difficult for schools in some areas to succeed.

As Margaret Maden has pointed out, 'it is important for schools to have "a 'critical mass' of more engaged, broadly 'pro-school' children to start with". We need to have schools that can meet the aspirations of all families and thereby provide that social and academic mix that has been shown to be essential for maximising the achievement of all children.

We know that there are already many comprehensive schools that perform with the best as far as academic achievement is concerned, while also doing many other things that private and grammar schools do not do. The aim must surely be to learn from those schools and help other comprehensive schools to do the same, rather than providing routes for pupils to escape from them. The broader problem of working class underachievement is barely addressed by the existence of privileged routes out for the few – and their very existence can serve to reduce the pressure for a more fundamental reform of provision.

Given the historic difficulties of achieving parity of

esteem between different schools, it is important that all schools see themselves, and are seen, as part of a comprehensive system of secondary education. To avoid diversity producing a hierarchy, all schools in an area need to work together in the interests of optimum provision for all pupils, including being willing to take a fair share of the more challenging pupils.

Beyond intakes

Even with fair admissions policies, a comprehensive system needs to go further and involves the creation of a comprehensive and inclusive approach to education within schools. The relationship between individual need and social entitlement requires careful handling if the point of having comprehensive intakes is not to be lost.

In this respect, and in others, both 'specialisation' and 'personalisation' have their dangers as well as their strengths. The original national curriculum may have been far too rigid, but the importance of a 'broad and balanced curriculum' remains. New arrangements for 14-19 education are long overdue, but they should not undermine the comprehensive principle by tracking students into pre-determined routes.

Successful comprehensive education also requires a closer relationship between education and other areas of social policy if disadvantaged pupils are to gain more equal opportunities. Multi-agency working between education, health and welfare services is essential throughout the system, not just in the early years, so we hope to see many more 'extended' schools as is now happening in Scotland.

Prospects for the future

Finally, we hope you will have noticed that some key

opinion leaders have been converted to the cause of comprehensive education. Former Observer editor, Will Hutton, for example, once regarded the lack of academic selection as damaging to Britain's global competitiveness and argued for the revival of grammar schools 'in order to attract members of the middle class back into the state system'. But by 2001 he was warning New Labour of the dangers of undermining comprehensive schooling.

In 2004, he cited a massively improved specialist comprehensive school in Hackney as showing 'the way forward for all our schools'. For him, it demonstrated that even a small increase in resources could lead to significant improvement and help challenge the hegemony of the private sector. Tellingly, he concluded with an appeal to his readers to send their own children to comprehensive schools and to demand that elite universities recruit more undergraduates from them.

We earnestly hope, Prime Minister, that you will put your own support behind that call.

Yours Sincerely

Geoff Whitty

Professor Geoff Whitty is Director of the Institute of Education, London University

Letter 6
Secondary school admissions and parental choice
Anne West

Dear Prime Minister

You say that you believe more parental 'choice' will empower parents, increase standards and improve the quality of education. But in reality, in rural areas it will make no difference, and in urban areas it will give more choice to middle-class parents of able children and less choice to parents who are disadvantaged and to those whose children are less able.

Whether the increase in 'parental choice' accounts for the improvements in educational performance in recent years is open to debate. What is clear though is that for many parents, there is no effective 'choice'. This is the case in rural areas. In urban areas and in particular in London, where there is, in theory, some choice, the increase in secondary school autonomy and independence has meant that it is often schools that choose pupils not parents who choose schools.

Allowing schools to become more independent and autonomous will not increase parental choice – rather it will increase the opportunities for schools to choose pupils. In England in 2000, research by Flatley and colleagues showed that over nine out of ten parents received an offer for their 'first preference' school. Parents in the shire counties were more likely than parents elsewhere to express a preference for their local school. In London, parents were the least likely to be offered a place for their child at the school they would 'most like'. The problem is acute in London as there is a higher proportion of autonomous schools (e.g. 'faith', 'foundation', 'academy') than in the rest of England, creating, as we shall see, particular difficulties.

Parents do not in fact make 'choices' – they rank their 'preferences'. The decision as to who should be offered a place at a school is taken by either the local education authority or, in the case of faith and foundation schools, by the school, although parents' ranking may not be taken into account by the admission authority. If the school does not have more applicants than there are places available all applicants are offered a place, except in the case of grammar schools. However, with popular schools, where there are more applicants than places, the school's published admissions criteria come into play. According to the 2003 DfES School Admissions Code of Practice these should be clear, fair and objective. This is where there is a major problem.

Most community comprehensive secondary schools and voluntary controlled schools have criteria that are clear, fair and objective. However, just under half of faith and foundation schools use at least one criterion that allows for a proportion of pupils to be selected by the school in question (e.g. on the basis of ability/aptitude in a subject area; via interviews with pupils/parents, giving priority to the child of an employee/governor, to a child with a family connection to the school). Moreover, my own research shows that far fewer faith and foundation schools mention giving priority to children with special educational needs or medical/social needs.

These differences can also help explain the problem

in London. Here, we find that there are proportionately more autonomous schools than in the rest of England; autonomous schools are more likely to select particular types of pupils, with the result that many appear higher in the league tables than community schools that do not cream and who admit disadvantaged children who are not admitted to autonomous schools.

Does this matter? In terms of social justice it does. Some children – those who are likely to do well in their GCSEs and enhance the school's league table position – are more likely to be offered a place at a popular faith or foundation school than others.

Research in which I have been involved shows that middle-class parents are more likely to apply to higher performing schools and their children are more likely to attend them, and that examination results are higher in faith and foundation schools than in community schools; given that the most important predictor of attainment is prior attainment this suggests a degree of creaming. Moreover, raw examination results, the focus of media attention, are even higher in faith and foundation schools with at least one selective admissions criterion.

In terms of social justice considerations, the percentage of pupils with special educational needs is lower in faith and foundation schools than in community schools. And if we look at the most selective schools, grammar schools, we find that a tiny minority of pupils are known to be from poor families. Finally, there is evidence from research by Stephen Gorard that greater diversity of school types is associated with greater segregation.

This is not to say that past Labour Governments have not made improvements. They have. There is now new legislation and a Code of Practice on School Admissions. There is an adjudicator to resolve local disputes in relation to school admissions. However, there is a problem with this form of quasi-regulation. The schools adjudicator is not proactive unlike regulatory bodies.

Another difficulty relates to the fact that the Code of Practice provides non-statutory guidance. A recent legal case has illustrated the effect of this. The current Code states that for admissions from September 2005 onwards day schools should not interview parents or pupils prior to admission. An objection to the Office of the Schools Adjudicator was made about the use of such interviews in one voluntary-aided school and the adjudicator directed the school in question not to interview prospective pupils and parents. However, the school governors successfully challenged the decision in December 2004. At the judicial review it was argued that the school had 'had regard' to the Code (as required) but then decided not to adhere to the guidance. The school governing body commented that had the government intended to ban interviewing it would have done so through primary or secondary legislation not via quasi-regulatory guidance – which of course raises the question, why not legislate?

A way forward

If schools are given more autonomy it is highly likely to lead to more creaming and more segregation. There is still a long way to go before children from disadvantaged backgrounds or who have special educational or medical needs have similar opportunities to access higher performing autonomous schools.

In conclusion, many autonomous schools act fundamentally in their own self-interest. They do not behave altruistically. Their admissions criteria are not designed to ensure that they take their 'fair share' of children with difficulties. Rather they use criteria and practices that enable them to give priority to pupils who are likely to benefit the school in terms of its league table position, and who are easier to teach.

This can be rectified by the new Government requiring all schools to use admissions criteria from a 'menu' of acceptable criteria as recommended by the Education and Skills Select Committee in 2004. Some form of 'controlled choice' should be considered as happens in parts of the US. In the English context, schools within an LEA (or group of LEAs) could be required to represent the balance in a given area in terms of either ability or poverty. Interestingly, before the 1988 Education Reform Act, there was a system of 'controlled' parental choice in operation in inner London. This used area-wide 'banding' by ability to try and ensure an intake to individual secondary schools that was truly comprehensive. In 1983, with this form of controlled choice, it was found that nearly 9 out of 10 inner London parents were offered a place for their child at their 'first preference' secondary school.

Moreover, whilst admissions are in the hands of individual schools, there will always be a concern that autonomous schools will not adhere to their published admissions criteria; many act in their own self-interest, not in the interests of the wider community or indeed in the interests of social cohesion. An independent body, with no vested interest in the outcome is needed to allocate pupils to schools on the basis of prescribed admissions criteria.

Only with a prescribed list and allocation being carried out by an independent body, can we be confident that parental choice will replace school choice on the basis of overtly, covertly or socially selective admissions criteria. For most community comprehensive schools serving their local communities, the notion that 'independence' will somehow improve standards has yet to be demonstrated. Changes need to be made on the basis of evidence, not on the basis of poorly implemented choice policies that allow for schools to choose pupils, not parents to choose schools.

Yours sincerely

Anne West

Anne West is Professor of Education Policy at the London School of Economics

Letter 7

A better deal for 14-19 year olds

Carol Adams, William Atkinson, Margaret Brown, Roger Brown, John Bynner, John Fowler, Margaret Maden, Geoff Melling, Chris Price and Ken Spour

Dear Prime Minister

We affirm, and hope you will agree, that the needs of employers, schools, colleges and parents are important matters in the development of education policy. The perspectives and needs of young people themselves are frequently assumed to be implicit in such discussions. Making these more explicit underlies much of what follows. A related matter is the underlying educational philosophy; the purposes of education - and training - in expanding the intellectual, social, cultural and spiritual capacities of all citizens.

We urge you to accept that in the development of policy and practice over the next 5-10 years, these aims should underpin all reform:-

- To increase radically the education and training participation of 16+ students, particularly those who currently drop out at age 17 (a particular problem in the UK, as OECD reports have shown) or are in the NEET (Not in Education, Employment or Training) group

- To identify from existing evidence, therefore, the conditions which create successful outcomes for those

50

who traditionally 'fail' and act on such knowledge,

- To secure for all 14-19 year old learners a range of entitlements which demonstrate principles of equity and quality with regard to curricular and resource provision,

- To provide a unified framework of programmes, courses, assessment and certification, built around a common core of skills, so that learners are offered maximum flexibility and 'second chances' if earlier educational experiences have been poor,

- To ensure that structural and governance arrangements support these aims, as well as other improvements sought in, for example, the Tomlinson Report.

The successful realisation of these aims requires an acknowledgement of the following issues and observations:-

More participation

There is already a wealth of research and evaluative data, as well as professional and institutional experience, which tells us a lot about why students 'drop-out' and, in relation to this, their preferred learning styles, their wider educational and institutional needs and the incentives which appear to underpin sustained engagement.

Well documented - and known by many teachers - are the strengths and weaknesses associated with recent experience of qualifications and examinations: Advanced GNVQ, CPVE, TVEI, AFL and Standard Assessment Tasks. These should be analysed and utilised in sorting out how different forms of assessment and curriculum design can contribute to student motivation and improved outcomes. Thus, it is understood that both summative and formative assessment are needed; each has its own rationale and purposes, exemplified over the past couple of decades in a host of programme developments. In this, as in other matters, policy amnesia and re-inventing wheels should be resisted.

We also acknowledge, from international as well as UK experience, that the signals emitted by the labour market and higher education directly affect young people's aspirations and risk-taking preparedness. Therefore, rhetoric about the value of 'less specialist' routes to gain access to higher education, or higher quality and longer vocational training, should be avoided if, in the former case, the more specialist routes are the more valued in practice and, in the latter case, early employment, without qualifications, is welcomed.

The success of EMAs (Educational Maintenance Allowances) for 16-18 year olds should be factored into the increased expenditure required for any strategy which is serious about higher participation for this age group when students and trainees are no longer required, by law, to partake of education or training.

Equity and Quality

We see equity and quality as being of equal importance. We value the traditional success and esteem associated with the 'A' level route and wish to see such success and esteem extended to other kinds of learning.

For this to happen, overly simple and retrograde distinctions between 'academic' and 'vocational' education have to be dropped. High quality vocational education, as in medicine or law, contains challenging theory and academic enquiry. Such principles should apply equally to early vocational programmes in school and college. Recent Adult Learning Inspectorate (ALI) concerns about the quality of teaching on vocational programmes need to be followed through with rigour, and also corrected.

Monitoring the progress of particular groups which are known to be ill-served by current provision is needed - for the whole of England, as well as at provider and funding levels. Thus, tracking the programme and institutional representation of young people in terms of their gender, ethnicity, special needs and socio-economic status should be mandatory. Where appropriate, funding allocations should be ear-marked for under- represented or under achieving groups, linked to projects designed and tested for such purposes.

Equity linked to educational quality also needs to ensure that the long-standing expectation in good schools that sporting, arts and voluntary service opportunities are intrinsic features of 'good education' should be extended to all young people. Good quality libraries, study centres (with PCs and inter/intranet access), and common rooms, should be widely available, as should pastoral and course guidance of high quality and independent of provider interests. Special tutorial support on a 'catch-up' basis is a further requirement, known to make a difference.

Such provision is as relevant to equity as it is to quality and directly affects the maintenance of student engagement and progress, as well as self esteem. How such an infrastructure is provided is a separate matter, normally in or between schools, colleges and workplace training centres. Overall, we believe, on the basis of evidence and experience, that stimulating and fulfilling young people's higher aspirations need to inform all the policies and practices which push for equity and quality.

A unified framework

For our first two aims to be secured, a unified framework - for curricular, assessment and certification purposes - is needed. We commend the Tomlinson proposals in this regard because the recommended structure allows young people to follow variable pathways or routes towards achieving a common Diploma, at four different levels.

Such a framework acknowledges the proper and real differences amongst and between 14-19 year olds whilst, at the same time, securing a highly desirable inclusivity of public certification. It is a welcome proxy for the US high school graduation 'rite of passage' and could become the norm, therefore, for 18 year-olds. Excluding ***A level students from this public affirmation of achievement is damaging to the majority of their peer group, with no evident benefit to the minority, except - perhaps - confirmation of historic status and exclusivity

Another characteristic of a unified framework which needs to be implemented - especially for the majority of young people who are currently ill-served by the system - is that of flexibility. Whilst there are limits to this in practice, we know that the 'zero currency' of some courses is damaging to many learners, with a rapid slither down one of several snakes occurring, and no available ladders back upwards. This is why 'credit transfer' is so important; when all or part of successful, but no longer wholly relevant study can be used for access to another pathway.

In the Tomlinson proposals, the unifying impact of the CKSA (Common Knowledge, Skills and Attributes) is welcome in this regard. Both content and assessment should be treated seriously and rigorously. It is important that all students, including those on Advanced level programmes, continue to develop their skills in the core areas of literacy and communication, mathematics and ICT, with no opting out before level 3 is attained.

System Structure and Governance

The increased diversity of curriculum, forms of assessment, certification, institutional bases and learners calls for a fresh look at governance and administration.

Irrespective of which developments may eventually emerge from the Tomlinson Report, it is clear that more collaboration across and between providers is necessary. Some of this will be so that students can maximise curricular opportunities in two, even three, institutions, school, college or workplace, and some will be at a more strategic level, to ensure that across a geographical area, there is sufficient and balanced provision and fair funding.

There will also be professional and cost advantages in having more managed or guided co-ordination in an area for in-service training, assessment consortia and pilot schemes for new curricula. Quality assurance will be linked to inspection with a virtuous circle of institutional and professional self assessment, external appraisal, feedback into development and improvement. Such a process is more likely to occur in a regional or sub-regional context than through more atomised national-institutional axes.

As schools become more autonomous and competitive - and in this phase, schools and colleges too - there is a greater need for some co-ordinating mechanism. Brokerage is required, without trying to revert to a mythical age of LEA 'command and control'. We are not convinced that LSCs are the right bodies for the purposes we outline here.

In the best interests of young people and, perhaps especially, those we have described earlier as not benefiting from current arrangements, we are strongly of the opinion that existing governance is wholly insufficient.

We believe that a degree of oversight and close co-ordination is needed for the following:

- Courses and curricula, securing a balance and range of specialisms.
- Careers and course guidance for students.
- Professional and curriculum development.
- Monitoring of input and output (student characteristics, equal opportunities, funding, certificated outcomes, etc).
- Funding (a mix of national norms and more local interventions arising from monitoring data).
- Inspection and quality control (a mix of national, OFSTED and relevant Skills Sectors, plus locally based agents of these).

Further, we would expect such devolved bodies to comprise representatives of providers, learners, employers, Trade Unions, Higher Education and Local and Regional Authorities.

Conclusion

We support the broad aims of both government aspirations and the Tomlinson Report. However, we urge the government to stand by the equal importance of equity and quality. There can be no convenient 'trade off' between these.

Separating out 'vocational' and 'academic' is profoundly damaging and short-sighted, Prime Minister. Such a split will simply confirm and deepen social, as well as educational divisions, and is intrinsically false. Future employment and a modern participative society require people who are adaptable and resourceful. Further, a 'well rounded education' is a universal entitlement and should not be regarded as something suited only to the few.

This overarching goal has financial, as well as curricular implications.

Yours sincerely

Carol Adams, William Atkinson, Margaret Brown, Roger Brown, John Bynner, John Fowler, Margaret Maden, Geoff Melling, Christopher Price, Ken Spour

Carol Adams is Chief Executive of the General Teaching Council

William Atkinson is Headteacher of the Phoenix High School

Margaret Brown is Professor of Mathematics Education at King's College, London University

Dr. Roger Brown is Principal of the Southampton Institute

John Bynner is Professor of Social Sciences in Education, Institute of Education, London University

John Fowler is an education consultant

Margaret Maden is Professor of Education, formerly Keele University

Geoff Melling is former Director, London Region Association of Colleges

Chris Price is former Vice Chancellor of Leeds Metropolitan University and former Chair of the House of Commons Education Select Committee

Dr Ken Spour is Reader in Education, Institute of Education, London University

A learners charter – 14-19
Margaret Maden

Dear Prime Minister,

I want to suggest that the context which frames learning is as important as curriculum, certification or even pedagogy. Students and apprentices have been surveyed widely and intensively and we now know a lot about the institutional conditions required for effective learning. Irrespective of a diploma framework, or a better deal for those who have traditionally under-performed or dropped-out, the day to day environment matters hugely. Overall performance will not be improved without some careful attention to this.

Whether the young person is in school, college or workplace training centre, we should ensure they are treated properly, with a serious sense of equity, justice and an acknowledgement that 14-19 year olds are emerging adults. This means they have rights, or entitlements, as well as duties, or obligations.

I therefore urge you to consider the need for a Learner's Charter, which acknowledges the importance of institutional norms to young people, whether in school, college or workplace. 'Context' comprises facilities, codes of conduct and expectations (for learners and staff), support services and the more indefinable issue of 'ethos' or 'climate' which affect the extent to which learners will stay the course and achieve their full potential.

Thus the construction of a more comprehensive and flexible curriculum and assessment framework needs to be supported and complemented by such a 'covenant' which expresses and articulates the nature of agreed assumptions as between the organisational provider and the learner.

In France there is 'la vie scolaire', in Sweden, the 'Student Barometer' and in most European countries, there are codified statutory rights - as well as responsibilities. Thus, learners in the upper secondary phase are clear about their role, as are teachers and instructors, as well as parents. Many schools and colleges in the UK have similar written agreements between older students or trainees and 'providers'. Whilst it is unlikely that in England such a Charter would be statutory but, rather, advisory, its components and principles should form the basis for proper - and ongoing - discussion between learners and provider institutions.

The Learner's Charter

Introduction: For all young people, ages 14-19, in school, college and work-based learning, there should be a written statement of expectations and responsibilities, applicable to both learner (including work-based trainees, school and college pupils and students) and provider (including schools, colleges and employers). This should also be available, for reference, to parents and authorised carers, as well as in prospectuses and other public information.

1   The expectations and responsibilities of providers would include:

1.1   An expectation that learners acquaint themselves with, and abide by, organisational rules relating to attendance, punctuality, work deadlines, plagiarism, assessment requirements, care and respect of property, health and safety procedures.

1.2   A mutual acceptance that both learners and teachers/instructors accept such organisational rules (above) and will, together, pursue the highest possible standards in these matters.

1.3   Provision of a disciplinary code, relating to both academic matters and general conduct, including periodic review with learners and an appeals procedure (for parents of students under age 16 and for students/trainees over age 16).

1.4   Ensuring that staff are appropriately qualified in their instructional and other roles.

1.5   Making available to each learner clear information, before enrolment, about course and organisational requirements and services. To include information about the staff assigned to agreed learning programmes and personal tutor (with contact details), sites and rooms, career and course guidance services, access to and scope of learning resources, learning support services, 'add-on' services and wider activities (e.g.: sports, arts, religious/faith practice facilities).

1.6   For each learner's work programme, the provision of adequately resourced instruction on no more than 3 sites, with facilities for social recreation and self-directed learning available, normally, 12 hours daily.

2.   The expectations and responsibilities of learners should include:

2.1   Having clear, written, information about:

- Work programmes and schedules, including assessment deadlines and criteria;
- Staff names and contact details;
- Organisational rules, including disciplinary procedures and appeals system;
- Feedback systems re: tuition and organisational matters;
- Services available both within the organisation and those provided elsewhere that are relevant to student/trainee welfare (e.g.: grants, social services, asylum seekers' support etc).

2.2 Agreeing to follow the organisation's rules, including its disciplinary and appeals procedures, respecting and looking after facilities provided, including social and catering services and areas.

2.3 Maintaining, with staff, the highest possible standards in relation to attendance, punctuality, meeting deadlines (e.g.: learners completing work assignments on time and staff returning such work, fully assessed, with advice, on time) and general conduct.

2.4 Being provided with adequately resourced instruction (e.g.: reliable access to equipment, books, computers, appropriate software, reasonably sized teaching groups) and support services (e.g.: learning resource centres, work-stations, learning support, career and course guidance etc).

2.5 Being allocated a personal tutor whose main responsibility is to co-ordinate and monitor the student/trainee's progress 'in the round' and, where appropriate, represent his/her interests to the organisation and the organisation's concerns to the student/trainee.

Conclusion

You will recognise, Prime Minister, that the charter's two sides, provider and learner, clearly reflect and echo each other. It is necessary that this is spelt out in quite formal terms although if the spirit underlying this - or any other charter - is negative or cynical, then learners will be conned. They will fail to make progress, in their studies, as well as in their growing adulthood. They, like their teachers and instructors, are workers and a charter should be centred on this reality.

At the same time, there remains a duty of care on the part of any learning organisation, stronger in a statutory sense with under-sixteens, but important to observe and understand beyond the legal frame. A charter of this kind is of growing significance and relevance as more and more young people move between sites and institutions for their study programmes. There should be a common set of expectations and duties across and between schools, colleges and workplace centres. It is most probably in the lower esteem courses that students are expected to move around most frequently. These are the students and trainees who are probably in greatest need of a fair deal and the level of consistency suggested in the charter.

What is described above is as applicable to 'high-fliers' as to under-achievers. In both categories there are learners who need to actively learn how to operate, in a more mature way, in their organisations. Staff also need to be clear about fair treatment to and by their students. What is implied and assumed in this charter clearly needs to be costed.

However, investment in decent quality study facilities, or in independent course and careers guidance, is a priority if higher levels of attainment are sought. Many such services require collaboration in a whole area, between schools, colleges and employers. Whatever means are used, it is the ends that eventually matter: namely, higher levels of achievement for all young people and better prepared and thoughtful adults and citizens in the 21st century.

Yours sincerely

Margaret Maden is Professor of Education, formerly Keele University

The needs of special education
Sally Tomlinson

Dear Prime Minister

Some of the most positive policies successive governments over the last thirty years have pursued have been those concerning children and young people with special educational needs and disabilities. It was a joint decision of Conservative and Labour governments in 1970 to bring severely disabled children - "the last to come in" - who had formerly been classed as ineducable, under the Department of Education. It was Mrs Thatcher, as Education Secretary who, in 1973, set up the Committee of Enquiry under Mary Warnock, which reported to a Labour government in 1978 that stigmatic categories of handicap should be abolished. This brought to public attention the view that larger numbers of children might at some time in their school career might have special educational needs and that all schools needed to take this into account.

It was a Conservative government that passed the 1981 Act that created the conditions for the integration of more and more children who had previously been segregated in separate schools and encouraged the inclusion of these children. It was a Conservative Act in 1993 that issued a Code of practice to LEAs and schools, with every school to appoint a Special Educational Needs Coordinator, and set up a Special Needs tribunal for parental appeals, and in 1995 passed a Disability Discrimination Act. It was a New Labour government in 1997 that placed the notion of "inclusion" at the centre of the educational agenda, and encouraged attempts to include as many children as possible within mainstream schooling.

Over its first term in office New Labour set out a framework for improving the quality of education for children with special educational needs. The 1997 Green Paper on "Excellence for All Children" and the 1998 Paper "Meeting Special Educational Needs - a programme for action" strengthened the rights of children to a mainstream education, although there was little recognition of the social and educational barriers that inhibited inclusion. Policy initiatives continued into New Labour's second term of office, with a revised Code of Practice and the Special Educational Needs and Disability Act in 2001.

This Act had historic importance as for the first time it linked special education needs with disability issues, a move disability rights activists had long been advocating. They had argued that segregated special educational institutions were part of an oppressive system creating barriers to full inclusion in educational, social and economic life. The most recent government strategy "Removing Barriers to Achievement" in 2004. links special educational need to the "Every Child Matters" agenda, and offers the possibility of integrated services, early intervention and embedding inclusive practices in all early years provision and all schools.

The questions for your new government, Prime Minister, centre around whether and how far inclusion is actually happening, and whether the wider policy agenda of continuing to set a diversity of schools in competition with each other actually works against the inclusion of those with special educational needs and disabilities.

On the first question, the "statementing" of children as having SEN increased slightly under New Labour - a 1% increase between 1999 and 2003, with noticeable local variation in statementing. Secondary school pupils were more likely to be statemented, with boys accounting for 77% of those with statements in secondary school. Differences between ethnic groups continued, Roma children and Irish travellers having the highest percentage of statements. African-Caribbean pupils, particularly boys, who had always been possible candidates for removal into some form of special education, continued to be excluded in disproportionate numbers into schools for the emotionally and behaviourally disturbed, into pupil referral units, and four times over-represented in straight exclusion from school.

The majority of pupils regarded as having learning difficulties, or being troublesome and disaffected in classrooms, and thus candidates for removal, are, as always, predominantly from lower socio-economic backgrounds, although you will know that some parents are happy to take advantage of statements for conditions such as dyslexia that bring extra resources or teaching time. Inclusion does not seem to work for all social and ethnic groups and this is an issue your government should address.

You may find that there are both old and new reasons for the reluctance of some schools and teachers to develop inclusive practices. It was after all, the practice of "payment by results" in the last part of the nineteenth century, that led teachers to exclude troublesome and hard-to-teach pupils into a standard zero class! As long as teachers are pressed to deliver higher standards in the form of more children passing examinations and reaching targets, they will understandably be reluctant to take on the education of all children.

There is also little time or incentive for teachers to

introduce new curriculum practices within mainstream schools, when the emphasis is on achieving at Key Stages and acquiring the magic five A-C GCSEs. For pupils who cannot ever achieve this, inclusive schooling is a sham. The idea of a meritocracy does not help either, children who find difficulty in getting a foot on the "ladder of opportunity" promised by Mr Blair, will always be at the bottom of a meritocratic society.

There is a major policy contradiction at the heart of current government policy which works against the notion of inclusive education. This is the policy of creating a market of schooling through choice and diversity on the assumption that it will raise standards for all. The evidence seems to point to the conclusion that while overt selection of pupils by "ability" and "aptitude" continues, there is much covert selection of the most and least "desirable" pupils. Those with special educational needs, or troublesome behaviour are not desired by many schools, and the polarisation of schools who take children with SEN and disabilities and those who do not, is likely to increase.

The integration of children's services and schools offering day-long educare sounds positive and cohesive, but you will need to guard against a further polarisation as selective schools and those in pleasant areas carry on as usual, while those in disadvantaged areas are the ones taking children with special needs and offering educare. Research funded by your Education Department has found that schools with higher levels of inclusion are the ones serving the more disadvantaged areas.

There are dangers too, in assuming that Colleges of Further Education will be able to take on more pupils with special needs and disaffection and "train" them from the age of 14, or that more troubled and troublesome pupils can be excluded from mainstream schooling into new kinds of "sin-bins". If you exclude large numbers of disaffected children into segregated units, schools or College courses, you may be training an underclass who will need "policing" in later life.

You will need to respond to groups of knowledgeable and sometimes vociferous parents lobbying for money for children diagnosed as autistic, and various other conditions. But it will always be expensive to fund separate provision and many of the children can be mainstreamed. You could also look carefully at the growing number of children and even University students claiming resources for dyslexia. Students should not be claiming to be dyslexic because they cannot understand Kafka. Please work with LEAs, Children's Centres and all schools to mainstream as many young people as possible and offer an education that will truly be inclusive. Separate segregated facilities are not the answer if you want to govern an inclusive, cohesive country.

Yours Sincerely

Sally Tomlinson

Professor Sally Tomlinson is a Senior Research Fellow in the Department of Educational Studies, Oxford University

Testing, testing, testing
Bethan Marshall

Dear Prime Minister

Children in England are now examined more than in any other country. The combination of national curriculum tests for seven, eleven and fourteen year olds, and major public examinations in the form of GSCE, AS and A2 levels at sixteen seventeen and eighteen, mean that only five years of formal education are free from either a major examination or an exam syllabus. During the course of their schooling the average pupil will sit just over one hundred public exams, around forty in the last three years. These test and examination scores form the chief accountability measure for school success through target setting and league tables. As such the stakes are high on all tests for both pupils and schools alike. As incoming Prime Minister you should be concerned by the extent and nature of the examination burden and seek to change it.

Evidence that the frequency of testing and the high stakes nature of the examinations is damaging the educational experience of the children in England is now overwhelming. I specify England because all other countries in the UK have now reduced the testing burden considerably. A major survey undertaken by Prof. John MacBeath for the National Union of

Teachers indicated that the tests have a distorting affect on the curriculum offered in the years of formal testing. His findings are supported by OFSTED. The chief inspector, David Bell, noted in his annual report that subjects other than English, maths and science are less well represented, particularly at the end of key stage 2. The arts and humanities suffer especially in the final years of primary education. Prof. Richard Docherty, who undertook a major review of the assessment arrangements in Wales, observed similar problems. He noted that the curriculum at key stage 3 was also affected by the nature of the tests at fourteen.

There are two reasons why the tests produce such a negative effect. The first is that, in order to ensure good results, teachers inevitably concentrate their efforts on that which is to be tested. In other words they teach to the test. The lack of correspondence between the educational process and teaching to the test has been noted since the inception of public education in this country.

In the nineteenth century, under the Revised Code, tests and inspection were combined – the inspectors tested the pupils – and schools were paid for their results. As with today, teachers were under huge pressure to make their charges perform. The poet and critic Matthew Arnold, who was also one of the first schools inspectors, observed in an inspection report, that "All test examinations may be said to narrow reading upon a certain given point, and to make it mechanical." He added that it "tends to make instruction mechanical and to set a bar to duly extending it ... [and] must inevitably concentrate the teachers' attention on producing this minimum and not simply on the good instruction of the school. The danger to be guarded against is the mistake of assuming these two – the producing of the minimum successfully and the good instruction of the school – as if they were identical".

There are economic precedents for the damaging effects of testing and using the scores as the basis for targets and accountability. Goodhart's Law suggests that rigid target setting can produce negative unforeseen consequences. The most commonly cited of these is that a target set to ensure the punctuality of trains is likely to produce more train cancellations. Similarly schools pressurised into producing high scores, to fare well in the league tables and meet targets, will concentrate their efforts on attracting those pupils likely to produce good results. They do so at the expense of a more comprehensive intake and pupils with special needs. League tables have also led, particularly at A-level, to schools taking off the school roll pupils unlikely to achieve highly. This creates a widening gap between the highest and lowest performing schools as there is little or no incentive to admit or keep challenging pupils.

The Macnamara Fallacy highlights the limitations of any measurement system. Charles Handy quotes it when suggesting that business needs to look beyond the profit margin to measure the success or otherwise of a company:

"The first step is to measure whatever can be easily measured. This is OK as far as it goes. The second is to disregard that which can't be easily measured or to give it arbitrary quantitative value. This is artificial and misleading. The third step is to presume that what can't be measured easily really isn't important. This is blindness. The fourth step is to say that what can't be easily measured really doesn't exist. This is suicide".

He summarises, "What does not get counted does not count", concluding, "Money is easily counted. Therefore all too soon, money becomes the measure of all things. A just society needs a new scorecard."

The Macnamara Fallacy leads us to the second cause of the damaging effects of testing – the nature of the tests themselves. For it is not only that the presence of such exams means that the arts and humanities are squeezed out of the primary school curriculum or that pupils specialise early in secondary school. The nature of the tests also distorts the curriculum being assessed. A study carried out by the Association of Teachers and Lecturers found that teachers believed, at all three key stages, that the tests restricted the teaching of the subject.

This is because, as the Macnamara Fallacy suggests, attention becomes concentrated on those items, which can be assessed in this form, namely timed examinations. Given the understandable tendency of teachers to teach to the test, only those elements of the subject which are easily measurable are covered. In subjects such as English this dramatically reduces the scope of the subject and therefore the validity of the assessment.

It also affects the type of learning that takes place in the classroom. A more passive, rote learning is encouraged as pupils cram for the test. Again economists, such as Diane Coyle, have noted that the constraints of the examination culture, and the limitations of its curriculum, ill prepare pupils for the demands of the new weightless economy. This they argue requires independent, active and flexible learners.

But perhaps the most worrying aspect of the current testing regime is the effect it has on the pupils themselves. Not only is their educational experience cramped by the frequency of the tests, there is evidence that it impacts upon their motivation, self-esteem and performance. The Assessment Reform Group undertook a review of the literature on the effects of testing and found that most were negative. Constant testing was found to have a de-motivating effect on pupils. In particular, children felt labelled from a very early age and this led them to limit their aspirations. Schooling becomes a series of hurdles every two or three years in which failure is reinforced for between a quarter and a half of the school population at each round.

Certainly we need schools to be held to account but raw test scores can and should only provide one element of the rich diversity of the work of a school. Given that we have known for nearly 150 years of the limitations of using examinations as an accountability measure, and the damaging educational consequences, we should look for an alternative system. It is important that the new government should make finding such an alternative a priority. Work already exists that might suggest a way forward.

There is now much independent research evidence that suggests that assessment can be a powerful lever to enhance the quality of pupils' learning. Work undertaken, amongst others by the research team at King's College London, demonstrates how assessment can be used to engage pupils in their own learning and reflect upon their progress. Rather than being something done to them it becomes a mechanism by which they achieve independence and, ultimately, perform better.

Assessment for learning, as it has come to be known, concentrates the attention of pupils and teachers alike on what can be learned rather than what has been learned, on future success rather than past failure. Although we must always have some of type formal, summative assessment of a pupil's achievement, we have currently got the balance between education and testing wrong.

As someone seeking to build a thriving economy for the future prosperity of the country you should wish to create an education system which encourages its pupils to be ambitious and active learners. You should wish for a curriculum that is sufficiently flexible that it can meet the ever-shifting demands of the global market and one that is satisfying to the learner for its own sake. At present we are encumbered with a testing regime which produces none of these ends. This must change if we are to give our children the education they both need and deserve. I urge you, therefore, to reconsider current policy.

Yours sincerely

Bethan Marshall

Bethan Marshall is Lecturer in Education, King's College, London

Letter 11
The future of further and higher education
Roger Brown

Dear Prime Minister

The period 1997 - 2005 has seen considerable Government achievements in both further and higher education but more remains to be done if Britain is to have truly world class education for all students after 16. Moreover the record of Britain's employers in providing training for the workforce remains patchy. However neither of the other main political parties has credible policies for dealing with these problems.

By far the most controversial issue in post-16 education, indeed in the whole of education, since 1997 was the introduction of variable tuition fees (from 2006). Although it is a pity that the Government rejected the Dearing Committee's 1997 recommendation for an income contingent contribution coupled with means tested grants, it deserves credit for accepting, in 2003, that this is the best way of levering in private funding, something which has already happened in the other Anglophone systems and which is beginning to be found even in continental Europe. The Government has also halted the slide in the funding of university teaching, considerably expanded funding for research, and put down a marker about the need for universities to increase their "third leg" funding. Greater priority is also being given to widening participation although the results so far are mixed.

In further education the creation of the Learning and Skills Council has led to greater coherence in funding and planning including work-based learning. Similarly the reorganisation of inspection has increased the effectiveness of the assessment of colleges' performance. As with higher education the decline in levels of public funding under the previous Government has been halted although the settlement for 2006 is a little disappointing. There is now much greater recognition of the key role that FE colleges play as well as much greater encouragement for them to get involved with local business. Finally, the Government has put its toe into the water on the issue of increasing private contributions.

Looking ahead, the main issues facing both sectors can be addressed under four headings: funding, structure, participation and regulation.

Funding

In spite of the progress since 1997 Britain remains towards the bottom of the OECD league table for spending on tertiary institutions. It is therefore vital that the increased levels of private revenues that will flow into the system after variable fees are introduced do not substitute for public expenditure (as has happened since 1998), and that levels of public funding per student are maintained in real terms. If this means that the achievement of the Government's 50% target is delayed beyond 2010 then that may be unavoidable, particularly if it also means a greater degree of stability in the system.

The Government will also need to give early attention to how the private funding is procured. The tuition fee has been capped at £3,000 with a review planned in 2009. There is a near universal assumption within higher education that the cap will not hold. £3,000 a student is considered far too little by the universities that see themselves as part of an international elite whilst others, particularly those that recruit large numbers of working class students, may struggle to attract home and EU students even at that level.

The Government should therefore give serious consideration to bringing forward the review, or even scrapping the cap altogether subject to certain provisos, notably requiring institutions that charge fees above the average cost of tuition – around £5,000 – to show that the additional revenues are being used to improve teaching and not being diverted into other activities such as research. The Government should also look again at the proposal for a national bursary scheme in place of the multitude of different local ones.

Finally, there is an urgent need to improve pay and conditions. Whilst a start has certainly been made with the Rewarding and Developing Staff Initiatives, there are not yet the resources in the system to enable the new pay framework to be properly implemented, and we are still a long way from the transformation envisaged by the Bett Committee.

Structure

In both higher and further education there is at present a considerable diversity of provision. But there is also a considerable diversity of funding. The most prosperous mainstream university (Imperial College) has a gross income for each full-time equivalent student more than eight times that of the least prosperous (the University of Lincoln). There are also significant differences in FE funding. Students studying A-levels in a school 6th form receive at least 10% more financial support than ones studying for the same qualifications at an FE college.

What these funding disparities mean is that there is in each sector an increasing hierarchy of providers. With private funding these hierarchies could become even more pronounced. The Government needs to consider whether this is in the interests of students and employers, and if it is not, what should be done about it. Ultimately it is very difficult to combine diversity with hierarchy.

Linked to this is the balance between competition and collaboration. Since 1997 the Government has been ambivalent, sometimes favouring increased competition, at other times wanting greater collaboration. In higher education, for example, the Government is concerned about the future of certain so called strategic subjects, which argues for collaboration, yet it has legislated for enhanced competition through tuition fees. Similarly in FE there is an emphasis on competition for enhanced status as Beacon Colleges, Centres of Vocational Excellence, Action for Business colleges etc, yet the Strategic Area Reviews often posit or require collaboration. The Government needs to consider how to create a greater cohesion in local provision. This may require the establishment of local machinery to co-ordinate the work of local providers to a greater extent than is currently the case.

A final structural issue is whether and how far institutions should specialise and if so, who should determine what the specialism should be. Whilst there is a clear case for greater and more effective co-ordination to address specific market failures, attempts to pigeonhole institutions by assigning them specific roles - for example, for schools to concentrate on academic subjects, colleges on vocational provision, and work-based learning providers on apprenticeships – will be bound to lead to sub-optimal levels of provision.

Participation

One area where there is already some institutional collaboration, but could be more, is participation in education particularly by students and employees with working class backgrounds. The problems here are mainly on the demand side, the result being that there are insufficient numbers of students coming forward with the appropriate qualifications for entry. The Government's decisions about the 14-19 curriculum and organisation will have far more bearing on this than universities' and colleges' responses, as will the success of its wider crusade against child poverty and the associated housing conditions.

Nevertheless there is more that could be done to encourage, reward and protect those institutions – some post-1992 universities and colleges and many general further education colleges – that see widening participation as a core part of their mission and that between them educate the great bulk of working class students, and indeed other minority groups. A good starting point would be to compensate them fully for the additional costs of providing for such students.

Another area that may require a modification of previous policies is skills creation. There is abundant evidence that the education and training of Britain's workforce leaves much to be desired in terms both of international competitiveness and employee development. Moreover much of this evidence is of long standing. While some employers train to world class standards, there are too many that provide little or no training for their staff but rely on other firms, or the state, to do their work for them. Although some financial incentives have been provided, in the main the Government's preference since 1997 has been to rely upon voluntary effort and co-operation. But the time may have come when the current variations in provision are considered unacceptable and employers be given targets for things like apprenticeships, work-placements and paid educational leave for their employees, perhaps in return for Government recognition or support.

Regulation

The final main issue for the Government in further and higher education is the level and kind of external regulation of universities and colleges. Here again there has been progress since 1997. A recent survey found a 25% reduction in the costs of external quality regulation in higher education whilst Sir George Sweeney's "bureaucracy busting" taskforce has led to some easing of the regulatory pressures on FE colleges. But in both sectors there is scope for more streamlining, building on the work of the Cabinet sub-committee on public inspection. In both sectors the aim should be for each provider to have one "lead" regulator with and through whom the necessary conversations about performance and the use of public funds should normally be conducted, as is already the case in some other parts of the economy.

Yours sincerely,

Roger Brown

Dr Roger Brown is Principal of the Southampton Institute

Letter 12

Widening participation in higher education

Carole Leathwood

Dear Prime Minister

The last Labour Government's stated commitment to widening participation in higher education is to be applauded. For far too long, a university education, with all the benefits that it brings, has been the preserve of the privileged, something that might have been acceptable in the late 19th and early 20th centuries but which is surely not appropriate for 21st century Britain. Higher education participation has certainly increased dramatically over that time period, with only 1% (of the age band) attending university in 1900, rising to approximately 8.5% in 1962, to 44% of 17-30 year olds in England in 2002-03, although the comparable figure for young people aged 18-19 was only approximately 30% in 2004. The 1997-2001 Labour Government's commitment to increase this further with a 50% target participation rate by 2010 was welcome. After all, Scotland has already achieved such a level of participation.

A number of policy initiatives have, therefore, been developed to widen participation, including: programmes designed to increase achievement in schools; measures to encourage partnerships between schools, colleges and universities; the reintroduction of some form of maintenance grant for the poorest students; and policies to encourage universities to embrace widening participation both by allocating specific funding to help to meet the costs of enhancing access and supporting students from under-represented backgrounds and by requiring universities to develop access strategies if they wish to charge top-up fees.

Yet, despite these initiatives, little has changed. Yes, more students from working-class backgrounds are attending university, but the vast majority of the increase in participation noted above has been from the middle classes, with the gap between the participation rates of the highest and lowest social classes as wide as ever. Social Trends (2004) reports that although the participation of young people from manual social classes increased from 11% in 1991-92 to 19% ten years later, participation rates of those from non-manual backgrounds increased from 35% to 50% over the same period. UCAS figures for 2003 show that almost 43% of all accepted applicants were from the managerial and professional classes, compared to a comparable figure of less than 5% from 'routine occupations' backgrounds. And whilst much has been made of the increased participation of women in HE, this has been middle-class women, with the participation rates for working-class women students not markedly different than for working-class men. It seems that higher education is still predominantly the preserve of the privileged.

And yet why, given the efforts that have been made to widen participation? One of the problems is that a number of government policies are contradictory, and some initiatives simply do not go far enough. The drive to increase achievement in schools to ensure that more young people gain the necessary entry requirements for HE is obviously important, yet differentiation between schools, which the government is further encouraging with the development of privately run academies, is likely to reinforce class differences and inequalities, as a report by

PriceWaterhouseCooper warned prior to the government's recent announcement of yet more academies. And social class remains a particularly powerful determinant of educational outcomes.

The reintroduction of the maintenance grant for poorer students is an important development, yet this is still lower than the grant available to students when the Labour Government came to power in 1997, and the introduction of fees and, now, of variable fees, threatens to undo any benefits derived from the grant system. Whilst the Government insists that the new fee regime has not resulted in a reduction in the proportion of applicants from working class groups, it has certainly not helped to increase participation from these groups, which is surely the aim, and the Education Maintenance Allowance has increased levels of post-16 participation. There is now a solid body of research, some commissioned by the government itself, which indicates that debt, and fear of debt is of far greater concern to poorer students, as well as to some minority ethnic groups, mature students and women. Top-up fees are not likely to reduce these concerns.

But it is not only the financial risks of university study that are greater for working-class students. The majority of working–class (and minority ethnic) students are concentrated in the post-1992 universities, i.e. in institutions which tend to have lower levels of prestige and funding than their research-intensive pre-1992 counterparts. This impacts on their future career and earnings opportunities, with research by Conlon and Chevalier in 2002 showing that students from the elite sector earn significantly more on average than those from post-1992 institutions, and continue to dominate the higher levels of government, the civil service and the judiciary.

Gender and ethnicity, as well as social class also

continue to impact on opportunities in the graduate labour market, with working class, minority ethnic and women students all likely to earn less on average. Government attempts to encourage participation on the basis of high average future earnings do not take these considerations into account, but research has shown that some working-class non-participants (and students) are aware of the hierarchy of universities and concerned that the universities they feel are open to them are less prestigious. The prospect of getting into a considerable amount of debt and possibly not getting a good job after graduation is a factor in some non-participants' reluctance to consider higher education study. This was not a case of 'low aspirations', but a rational and considered response to risk.

It is also evident that some working-class young people do not consider university to be a place for them, hence the numerous projects, such as summer schools, designed to change this perception. Again, such projects have a place, but until universities themselves challenge their exclusive practices and cultures, which many working-class people regard as 'snobbish' and alien, such projects will have limited success. Working–class young people do not necessarily want to have to change who they are, or to lose their sense of identity, in order to be able to benefit from university study. It is not enough, therefore, to concentrate only on access to university; rather it is important to consider the kinds of university experience available and the opportunities that are likely to accrue from that. Many working class and minority ethnic students positively choose post-1992 institutions where they expect to find more students like themselves and to be more likely to fit in.

Yet when such institutions have fewer resources, with, for example, poorer staff-student ratios and fewer library resources, such students may well be at a disadvantage in relation to their peers at more prestigious institutions. Policies designed to enhance institutional diversity are likely to further reinforce the hierarchy of funding and prestige, where, just like in schools, those students who go to the 'top' universities will benefit at the expense of those who go to universities lower down the institutional league tables. And whilst those institutions with the most 'non-traditional' students have benefited most from the (limited) government funding provided to support widening participation, the increased concentration of research funding in the elite institutions has meant that the resource gap between institutions has not reduced and in some cases has widened. Roger Brown has argued that in a variable fees market, it is precisely those institutions with the most widening participation students who are most at risk financially.

It is also not good enough to assume, as Margaret Hodge announced in April 2002, that widening participation 'means expanding vocational courses; it means developing foundation degrees; it means developing sub-degree qualifications'. The implication here is that the new higher education students, those from working-class backgrounds, are to be steered into sub-degree and vocational programmes, rather than able to access the more prestigious academic degree courses. What also underlies this is an assumption that this is what these students are best suited to.

The class prejudices evident here do not belong in the 21st century. When vocational courses achieve parity of esteem with academic ones (something that is also critical to debates about the 14-19 curriculum), and when participation in vocational, sub-degree and academic degree programmes ceases to reflect social class differences, but is reflective of the broader diversity of society – then we can begin to talk about widening participation in terms of expanding vocational and sub-degree provision.

So what is needed to widen, rather than simply

increase, participation? A major priority must be to tackle the socio-economic inequalities that produce educational inequalities in the first place. This necessitates redistributive policies to tackle poverty, low pay and poor housing, alongside educational policies that ensure that all children and young people, not just those from privileged backgrounds, are able to attend a good, well-resourced, local school. This would do more to raise the achievement and HE participation of under-represented groups than policies of choice, selection and institutional differentiation.

However unpalatable for a government to swallow, debt and fear of debt is likely to remain a major deterrent for working-class students. The issue of fees and student finance therefore needs to be re-visited. Policy also needs to be directed at producing a less hierarchical system of higher education, with all institutions adequately funded for teaching and research to reduce the prestige and funding gap between institutions at the top and bottom of this hierarchy. This would help to ensure that an excellent higher education experience is, to use an oft-quoted phrase of the last Government, available to the many, not just the few.

A university education is something that many of us cherish and have greatly benefited from. Let's not deny that opportunity to others.

Yours sincerely

Carole Leathwood

Carole Leathwood is Senior Research Fellow, Institute for Policy Studies in Education, London Metropolitan University

Letter 13

Falling in love and staying in love with lifelong learning

Frank Coffield

Dear Prime Minister

Welcome to 10 Downing Street and the first avalanche of advice on what you should do. Instead of bowing to the 'tyranny of momentum' (a phrase coined by Peter Hyman to summarise the battle between government and the media for the political agenda), may I suggest a period of quiet reflection before you formulate any new policies or take any decisions? In my view, it's the first requisite of a new administration to build on the successes, and to learn from the failures, of its predecessors. It's not, however, self-evident which are the successes and which the failures, because these judgements need to be based on evidence rather than assertion; and, because of years of neglect, we've a poverty-stricken research base on which to make judgements about post-16 learning.

Many previous initiatives have either been only partially evaluated; or not evaluated at all; or are virtually impossible to evaluate, because they're operating alongside another 40 to 50 initiatives in the same field (I kid you not); or they've been evaluated by consulting firms who, for tidy sums of public money, have produced the findings governments want to hear. (You may pretend surprise at this, but we all know it goes on.)

I can offer you advice on only one part, but a highly important though frequently neglected part, of the education, training and employment 'system' (to use that term loosely), namely, lifelong learning (LLL). I should warn you right from the start: LLL (or 'Big L', as I like to call her) is a very demanding mistress, because she insists we all learn from our past actions, reflect critically on the quality of our current thinking and consult relevant partners about our future plans.

She's not impressed, for example, by the fact that since 1997 we've had 7 Ministers of LLL in 8 years: it doesn't really show commitment, does it? She has not been made a high priority despite all the hype. No wonder the woman's distraught. You come from a political culture wedded to the short-term, to an initiative a month, all of them tied to the careers of thrusting ministers desperate to make their mark. But she wants a long-term commitment, does Big L, not one night stands or even one year stands. Half in jest, could I suggest you appoint a Lifelong Minister of Learning? Or at least a Minister of Learning who stays in post for a full four years? Not exactly a lifetime, I admit, but it would be a start.

I say half in jest but I'm wholly in earnest because Big L's insistence that we all get better at learning applies to prime ministers as well as to doctors, teachers, employers, trade unionists, apprentices and professors of education. I guess the most difficult thing for you to learn, as the newly elected Prime Minister, is that some of your favourite policies and your leadership style can become part of the problem. For instance, a national target of getting 50% of each generation into universities is having the unintended consequence of new graduates filling the jobs usually taken by those whose highest qualification is Level 3 (A levels or equivalent), because the graduates can't find graduate jobs. When half of each generation are in the race for a declining number of highly skilled jobs, then the competition is going to become fierce. University fees only serve to eliminate from the competition children from families with relatively modest means. We need to improve the quality of many jobs, and the quantity of good jobs, as well as close the widening disparities between the regions.

The quickest way of showing you're capable of learning would be to announce that policy will from now on be developed in collaboration with those who have to implement it; and not developed by bright young things (who've never taught in an FE College and who can't tell their ALI from their OFSTED). Imposition from on high doesn't work anymore: ask football manager Graeme Souness or, better still, the player with whom he quarrelled, Craig Bellamy. Big L would also like you to enlarge your repertoire: one position is boring and she's fed up with Lone Crusaders attempting to transform public services by pouring policy texts (and initiatives) over the professionals, who haven't got time to read them, never mind implement them. A Learning Society will not be created in this country by an endless stream of policy documents, about which no-one has been consulted until they've been issued and often not even then.

So it means from now on fewer photo-opportunities, fewer publicity stunts, fewer initiatives, less (but better) legislation, and more genuine consultation and participation by the professionals. Partnership does not mean that the practitioners 'deliver' locally the policies you have decided on centrally.

In the rush to introduce 'Personalised Learning', which may turn out to be a good idea, please don't make the mistake of involving learners in the reforms, but excluding their teachers / trainers. Teaching and Learning are the two sides of the same coin and you're wasting effort trying to split hard currency in two. Drop any prejudices against teachers; see them as allies and help them become experts in teaching and learning. (I know. It will be hard for you.

Big L is tough to live with, but she'll make you a better person and a better PM, I promise.)

After eight years of New Labour, Big L feels, well, not rejected, but misunderstood. She doesn't want to be just another addition to the harem (the divisions within the DfES and within educational institutes). She wants to be taken seriously in her own right. She wants to reform the whole system, the whole household. She wants to break down the walls between the rooms, and get Early Years talking and working 'seamlessly' (I love that adverb) with Primary, Secondary, Further, Higher, Adult and Work Based Learning. Big L won't believe you're serious about her until you alter the organisational structure of the DfES to reflect her overarching significance.

Only then will students be able to progress and stay in touch with her throughout their lives. She wants all students leaving school not only to have heard about her, but to have fallen in love with her and to carry a torch for her until the day they die. She wants adults in work and out of work, at home, in the community and in retirement to be just as keen on her and to come back to see her regularly. She doesn't want people who are keen to learn turned away because of your obsession with tests and measurement. She wants to be loved for herself and not just for the certificates you force her to hand out. She doesn't want people to pretend to love her, she's offering the real thing, the Big R, a lifelong relationship.

If you're to treat her as she deserves, it means fundamental change, and it should start at the top with you. It's called being a Role Model. She loved the noble and inspiring tribute that David Blunkett paid her in 1998 (". . . helps make ours a civilised society"). His rhetoric is memorable, but too many of his policies were frenetic, top-down, heavy-handed, ill-considered and narrowly economic.

Big L's had enough of pretty words which are at

variance with the rough behaviour of those who enforce their utilitarian reading of Blunkett's vision on the rest of us. She suspects you're just using her humanistic appeal to legitimate authoritarian policies and she's adamant: compulsory Lifelong Learning is a contradiction in terms. Heavens, she doesn't need people to be forced to love her. What an insult. She also reacts very badly, as we all do, to 'cascade bullying', which vividly describes how government policy is being enacted in too many Universities, FE Colleges and Schools.

The previous government's handling of the Learning and Skills Council (LSC) is an example of the Crackerjack School of Performance Management, so named after the TV programme where contestants were loaded with more and more cabbages until they dropped one. Burdening the LSC with more and more roles and responsibilities suggests that it is being set up for failure. It deserves a chance to succeed.

She'd also like you to be more courageous. Be radical. If your ideas don't move forward, they'll start calling 10 Downing Street the Stationary Office. The previous government claimed to be modernisers, but was in fact wedded to the past, as its timorous response to the Tomlinson Report demonstrated. You must not be concerned only about educating future leaders, while high proportions of young people continue to leave education with precious little. So don't be scared of frightening the horses or the middle-classes, or even the middle-class horses.

There are some big boys in the playground who, frankly, do as they please. They call themselves The Employers or the CBI for short. They're widely feared, but most are big pussy-cats close up – they just think that individual motivation will solve the problems of poor, teenage mums or adults struggling to get by on the minimum wage or ethnic minorities being discriminated against.

The best employers are only too well aware that their

workers need Big L if they are to maintain or enhance their jobs. But there are far too many of them in the UK who are quite happy to see public sector employees under the cosh, because, while government is absorbed in putting the stick about, they're moving the jobs to India or China.

Prime Minister, on behalf of the whole community, Big L wants you to stand up to those who fail to train their employees properly or at all, who don't appreciate the value added by Union Learning Reps, or who walk out on communities whose workers have provided their profits for generations. Introduce Paid Educational Leave for all employees and set some targets for employers (yes, employers) to improve the quality of their goods and services.

If you want to surprise Big L, base all your Lifelong Learning policies on social justice; that alone will make you stand out from all the other boys. Please don't rabbit on about "a step change to a demand-led system", there are already four definitions of what that ugly jargon means.

If you want a really big idea for a third term, let's learn from the Japanese vision of lifelong learning. For them, it's certainly not just about plugging skills gaps. It's also more than reforming the education and training system or their Department of Education. They want to reconstruct their whole society by interpreting lifelong learning as the building of local communities. Magic. A statue to Big L in every town and village.

As I said, Big L's a hard task mistress. She has not been tried and found wanting: as she's been found to be demanding, she has not been tried at all. But, Prime Minister, please fall and stay in love with her. You'll have a ball. Cinderella will be transformed into a Princess, the pumpkin ... no, I must resist temptation. Provided there's sufficient public and private investment in research and development, Big L will do her bit to enliven, educate and enrich (spiritually, intellectually and financially) all of us, and she'll also transform us into engaged citizens. Go on, PM, give her a kiss: you never know, you might get to like it.

Yours sincerely,

Frank Coffield.

Frank Coffield is Professor of Education at the Institute of Education, London University

Getting serious about achievement and racism
David Gillborn

Dear Prime Minister,

I am sure that there are many pressing issues that you will be focusing on in the coming years but I would like to remind you of one that seems to have slipped off the radar of educational policymakers. Namely, the achievement of minority ethnic pupils, especially those groups who currently achieve below national averages in their GCSEs (that is, young people of African Caribbean, Pakistani and Bangladeshi ethnic heritage).

I am surprised that you have not made this issue a central part of your education plans. After all, we know a good deal about certain school-based processes that (often despite good intentions) can have the effect of disadvantaging young people from certain backgrounds. I am saddened that politicians often fall into the trap of assuming that poverty and language skills are the main barriers to learning for minority children. Although that view fits with long established stereotypes there is now considerable evidence to show that the education system itself inadvertently creates additional barriers for some groups: for example, by using testing regimes that discriminate against certain groups; by enforcing a narrow and imperialistic curriculum; through low teacher expectations; and, perhaps most shocking of all, the use of selective pupil grouping (so-called 'setting by ability') which is known to systematically disadvantage Black students and yet is practised more and more frequently and with ever younger groups of children.

I am especially disappointed by many politicians' stance on the matter of exclusions from school. I realise that looking 'tough' may play well with certain newspapers but, once the white heat of the campaign is over, could we please return to the Black reality of exclusions? For as long as data have been gathered on this matter it has been clear that Black pupils, especially those categorised as 'Black Caribbean' are considerably more likely to be excluded from school than their white peers of the same sex and social class background. I have been impressed by rhetoric on dealing with inefficiency in the public services; perhaps you can see how exclusion from school is yet another form of wasted of potential (not to mention the sheer injustice of the present system)?

This situation has been allowed to persist for too long. I am sure that you will wish to make this a key priority for your coming term, unless, that is, you care less for social justice and inclusion than for the 'freedom' of headteachers to end prematurely the educational careers of young people. By the way, OFSTED has documented the unfairness of the present system, and surveys of Black parents reveal that this is one of their main concerns when it comes to education.

Finally, I would like to congratulate you on your firm position on law and order. As you have so rightly noted, on several occasions, the mark of a truly free and democratic society is that the law is respected and applied without fear or favour. Consequently, I would like to remind you of the Race Relations (Amendment) Act 2000 and the binding legal duties that it placed on more than 45,000 public institutions – including the key offices of government.

You will recall that the amended race relations legislation arose as a direct result of the Stephen Lawrence Inquiry. I am sure that you remember Stephen Lawrence. An 18 year old young man; a dedicated and ambitious student who wanted to be an architect; a well liked friend and cherished son, who was brutally murdered on a London street for the 'crime' of being Black. He was stabbed to death by a group of white racist youths and left lying in the street. The attending police officers checked for a pulse but did nothing to stem the flow of blood. A 14 year old girl who witnessed the scene was amazed that no action was taken but the police officers assured the subsequent inquiry that their failure to act was a result of their inadequate training, not any racism on their part.

Politicians expressed its outrage at the murder and pledged that racism has no place in Britain. The amended race relations legislation helps to move us towards a more just Britain by making public institutions face up to their own responsibilities in this field and state-funded schools face a series of specific requirements. Every school, for example, must have a written race equality policy; they must monitor their activities for any sign of bias (including pupil achievements and staff recruitment/retention); and they must plan for improved race equality in the future. These are admirable measures that would probably have a marked impact on the education system if we could seriously believe that they are being observed.

Unfortunately, it is not clear that most schools even have a written policy yet. Evidence gathered by the Commission for Racial Equality suggests, in those schools that have a policy, in most cases it does not set any meaningful targets for change. Furthermore, people working in education are amongst the least positive about the impact of any race equality changes that they have seen to date. Worse still, those in schools are the least likely to feel in need of any further guidance on these issues.

Put bluntly, many schools appear to be relatively inactive in their duties under the law and uninterested in making any further progress. I realise that blaming the school children and/or their parents would be a convenient way out of this situation but can such a view really be sustained any longer? The law of the land requires schools to take positive action to ensure that they are not discriminating (either deliberately or unwittingly): can you really allow schools to flout this law any longer?

I realise, of course, that school teachers are busy. Headteachers are busy. School inspectors are busy. You are busy. I am sure, however, that none of the aforementioned people are too busy to do their part in helping to ensure that every child gets a fair chance in school regardless of their ethnic origin.

I look forward to your government placing this at the centre of its education policies in the near future.

Yours sincerely

David Gillborn

David Gillborn is a Professor at the Institute of Education, London University

A new partnership between teachers and government?

Bob Moon

Dear Prime Minister,

You could almost touch the mood of euphoria in school staffrooms on May 2nd 1997. It was more than just party politics. A majority of teachers had become disillusioned by government policies, particularly after 1988. They weren't necessarily against some of the ideas (national curriculum, local management of schools). They were, however, totally opposed to the way their views on the reforms were ignored and sometimes publicly spurned. Some big mistakes were made. Hundreds of millions of pounds, for example, wasted during the introduction of the national curriculum and assessment systems.

Teachers had good reason to be optimistic. In December 1995 Tony Blair and David Blunkett had launched the Labour party's 'Excellence for Everyone'. They talked about 'A new deal for teachers' and the expectations of a positive relationship between teachers and government were high. The euphoria was short lived. Labour's first policy moves were highly centralist, lacking even a veneer of consultation. Too many teachers gained the impression that they were seen as the problem, not the solution. Whilst teachers have gained some benefit from the extra resources given to education, they felt outside the reform setting agenda.

An ambivalence, even distrust, towards teachers has resonated through recent governments (Labour and Conservative). It was nowhere more starkly portrayed than in the juxtaposition that was set up in and between the then OFSTED Chief Inspector, Chris Woodhead, and the Chief Education Officer of Birmingham, Tim Brighouse, when Labour returned to power. In the very first days of power Downing Street moved to ensure that Woodhead, rather than Brighouse, was the Downing Street touchstone. Woodhead was, and is, reviled by teachers for his apparently arbitrary and personal attacks on the profession. Brighouse believes in challenging but gaining the trust of teachers. Just how significant pro teacher policies can be is illustrated by the little short of miraculous improvement in standards in Birmingham schools. And now the same 'Brighouse Approach' is paying huge dividends in London. Secondary schools in the capital in 2004 were above the national average for GCSE results!

There was a rawness and urgency in Labour's first term of office that reaped important rewards (the focus on literacy in the primary school, the challenge to expectations at secondary level), but at a price. Labour became seen as authoritarian and unfriendly to teachers. Professionals (like most workers) don't respond well to coercion. Young people do best with teachers they like and respect. Teachers are no different.

My impression is that, in a number of areas of public policy, government has been moving to a more inclusive, less dirigiste approach to decision making. I hope this continues and that it extends to teachers.

Assuming this, I want to suggest five ways in which the relationship between teachers and government could be improved.

First, we now have a centralised education system and it has been used as such (see my second point). It follows that what you and your ministers say is highly significant. If you talk up government education successes, then talk up the teachers too. Address them directly. There may be moments for velvet gloves and iron fists, but think carefully about motivation and morale. We have a million teachers in this country (half of whom are not teaching) and their views count. Research in England shows that the vast majority of parents think highly of their children's school. But they think the education 'system' is poor, even faulty. Just as a headteacher is responsible for how a school is perceived, so a Prime Minister and Education ministers have to bear responsibility for perceptions of the system as a whole.

Second, the centralism cannot be sustained. We have in Britain what might be termed an 'immature' system, with none of the checks and balances that makes mature centralised systems more responsive and judicious in coming to decisions. A French Education Minister has to take account of key interests and, frustrating as this can be, I believe it makes for a stronger basis for reform. In England (not Scotland, and less so Wales and Northern Ireland) a few political changes of mind in a matter of days amongst a handful of people in Whitehall can shift policy for 25,000 plus schools. It's a process that leads to mistakes and misunderstandings. Very few people are sharp enough to develop well founded policies at that pace.

My third point stems from the second. Many challenges remain for our school system. Lasting solutions will rarely come from central control. We need genuine innovation to return (not of the state sponsored variety) and that will mean giving teachers and communities the opportunity to explore over time imaginatively different forms of schooling. I believe, for example, that whatever the outcome of the plans for 14–19 education, the motivational and attitudinal problems of some students will only be addressed by allowing such licence.

Fourthly, despite a lot of rhetoric, teachers' professional development remains impoverished and inadequate. Whilst initial training has been significantly improved, the more crucial in-service support remains neglected. Only a few LEAs appear to do this well. Many are too small to provide intellectually challenging support. Links with universities are patchy and rarely gain a mention in the few government pronouncements on teacher development. Teachers question the quality of some of the unregulated private provision. More than 30 years ago there was a really interesting attempt to address this through a commission led by Lord James of Rusholme. The recommendations on professional development came to little. We need a wide ranging inquiry to provide us with a contemporary James Report for the 21st century.

Finally something needs to happen about the General Teaching Council (GTC). Labour failed to create a GTC that, in the words of the 1995 Excellence for Everyone 'gives full recognition to the professional status of teachers'. I think that, at the level of educational politics, it has been expedient to keep the GTC (and the teacher unions) on the sidelines and give greater rein to what, I believe, some officials see now as the more effectively run Teacher Training Agency (TTA). The future of the GTC, however, could be a crucial issue to test out a commitment to more devolved, more broadly based and more teacher friendly policies. The GTC as it operates today is marginal to most teachers' lives. There have been few issues on which it has been allowed to lead. But rethinking and rejuvenating the GTC (or perhaps democratising the TTA) might touch the imagination of teachers. The best policy comes from partnership between politics and people. Teachers need a forum for that to happen.

Yours sincerely,

Bob Moon

Bob Moon is Professor of Education at The Open University

Letter 16
The central role of local authorities
Dave Wilcox

Dear Prime Minister

Over the years, the relationship between central and local government has been variable. But, despite the lack of confidence sometimes displayed by Ministers in the capacity of local authorities, they have consistently acknowledged the unique importance and legitimacy of councils' role in the delivery of public services to local communities.

The manner in which that role is performed has been subject to constant change, and few institutions have shown themselves to be so adaptable, or so willing to rise to the challenge of improving provision to meet the very diverse needs of those whom they serve, and to whom they are accountable. That is particularly true of the way in which local authorities have responded to the shifting, and sometimes not entirely coherent, demands in respect of education and children's services. Their role remains central to the successful achievement of improved outcomes for the whole community: better, more widely available childcare; higher attainment levels for learners across the age range; improved outcomes for children, young people and their families in health, social and economic well being. Not to mention a matching range of expectations in respect of adult members of the community, including the growing proportion of elderly.

There have been major changes in the way that authorities perform this role. No longer the monopoly provider of a wide range of services to largely acquiescent recipients, councils are instead at the heart of an increasingly complex web of partnerships – of other providers and agencies, and of consumer and community groups in a variety of guises. While retaining a role as major providers of some services, they are now commissioners, brokers, community champions, quality assurors and – crucially – strategic leaders in their localities.

In this new approach, children's service authorities are required to have a Director and a Lead Member for Children's Services. With a view to improving a range of outcomes for children, young people and their families (specifically the five Every Child Matters outcomes now laid down in statute), they are responsible for promoting partnerships between the Council and other local providers and agencies who (with the notable and controversial exception of schools and general practitioners) are under a legal duty to co-operate.

New Local Safeguarding Children Boards must be established (a key role for Lead Members) and an overarching single Children's Services Plan must be drawn up. It is necessary to bring in other partners whose activities have a significant bearing on educational, social and economic well being: for example, other council departments (regeneration, housing, leisure, libraries, etc.), a range of voluntary/community sector organisations, local business and others. A key feature of success for these arrangements will be the ability to work productively with a wide range of other professional and representative leaders – including those with no matching statutory obligations. There is also a requirement to involve the recipients of services in their development.

If they are to succeed, however, the conditions for exercising strategic leadership in such a complex and demanding environment must be in place. Ultimately, responsibilities must be backed by powers but, just as importantly, councils need the same high level of credibility as other leaders if they are to take their communities with them. They must, of course, earn this for themselves – but they must be given the opportunity to do so without being held back by central government. For too long, both government and opposition have implicitly, and sometimes explicitly, undermined the standing of local government. Powers have been whittled away; local autonomy has been diminished by the imposition of central targets and strategies; performance has often been questioned to an exaggerated degree; and there has been a lack of clarity and consistency about the role expected of local councillors. There have been several manifestations of a move towards neighbourhood initiatives, often with good intentions, but too frequently with the appearance of by-passing elected local councillors – whose views sometimes seem to count for far less than those of other interest groups.

In education, the last few years have seen a significant increase, for sound educational reasons, in the autonomy of schools – responding to the recognition that it is schools themselves that must be responsible for their own performance, and thus for delivery of the improved standards which are the shared objective of all. But in some respects, and in some quarters, autonomy appears to have become an end in itself, regardless of the effect on the overall system of provision or the impact on some of the most vulnerable groups of learners; regardless also of the difficulty this might cause local authorities in leading the change that is now expected of them, and upon whom those groups largely depend to protect and promote their interests. The period leading up to this latest general election has been marked by an acceleration of that tendency.

For example, the possibility of coherent strategic planning of school places to meet the needs of all is put at risk by enabling some schools to expand regardless of the impact on others. The emphasis on choice belies the extent to which the gains for some will reduce the options for others. The growing clamour around poor behaviour threatens to transmit the problem from more advantaged institutions to those which are not in a position to pick and choose, and diminishes the prospect of satisfactorily resolving the issues. The duty on local authorities to promote the educational achievement of looked after children is not matched by a similar duty on schools. Indeed, over-subscribed schools are under no effective pressure to admit either this or any other 'hard to place' group of vulnerable children seeking places outside the main transfer round from primary to secondary education (when the majority of such cases arise). Whilst inspectors will now report on how well schools contribute to the five well being outcomes of children, this means for their own pupils not the children of the local community – which, all too often, is a very different proposition.

It is time for a change of attitude from senior national politicians. There have been signs of significant change in some quarters, particularly amongst those with responsibility for local government, but there is much residual ambivalence in other departments. Central and local government agree about the importance of strong and effective local leadership; both the ODPM and LGA published papers on the issue earlier this year. There is also shared concern about securing the future supply and development of local political leaders, especially the difficulty of attracting into local government as councillors a properly representative range of individuals with the qualities and desire to make a real difference to their communities; many currently choose other outlets for their energy and talents, without progressing into democratic politics. The current profile of local councillors (of which I am an example) is older and much whiter and more male than the population as a whole. This also undermines the credibility of councils as representatives and leaders of their communities.

Boosting the performance, the perception and the representative nature of local authorities must be a shared objective across Westminster and Whitehall, and in town and county halls. In no area of policy is this more important than in education, and in none are there such prospects of creating a potentially virtuous circle – particularly with the additional element of the cross-cutting approach required to meet the demands of the broader children's services agenda. Indeed, this brings not only the need for a high level of credibility, but also creates the opportunity for engaging a wide range of individuals throughout the community – service providers and users – in a manner which, if the experience is positive, could encourage them to consider seeking a broader role in representative politics.

Many local authorities have demonstrated consistent success for decades; others have contributed many innovative improvements to the delivery of services. This, of course, is not the stuff of headlines. Yet even those with shortcomings have markedly improved their performance in recent years, conspicuously in education – where, admittedly, they have been put under considerable pressure; but they have mostly responded well, as the evidence of subsequent inspection makes clear. Now, authorities across the land are energetically and enthusiastically engaging in the new approach to children's services.

This is a promising demonstration of the leadership that will need to be extended far more widely, but the whole endeavour will be jeopardised without a more whole-hearted commitment from every part of the political establishment – particularly, it must be said, from the very top.

It appears to be a policy shared by all parties that every child matters – the title of the Green Paper from which the children's services agenda springs. However, on a number of fronts, while credit is sought for promoting the interests of the most disadvantaged, this is truer in rhetoric than in practice. It is seldom that significant benefits for the most needy are proposed if doing so is perceived to threaten the interests of the more advantaged. When it comes to 'tough decisions', harsh political reality – the prospect of being punished at the ballot box by those more likely to vote – too often appears to outweigh the moral purpose which should underlie education policy. There is a real need for national political leaders to articulate more clearly the importance of establishing a system of provision in which every child really does matter, in order that local authorities can successfully play their central role in leading such a change at community level.

Yours sincerely,

Dave Wilcox

Councillor Dave Wilcox is Chair of the Local Government Information Unit

Bridging the public/private divide
Chris Price

Dear Prime Minister

The present government's policies for secondary schooling have been described by some as 'privatisation'; this is not strictly accurate in that there have been no proposals so far to enable schools maintained by the taxpayer to charge fees – which were made illegal 60 years ago. Many secondary schools, however, (including the London Oratory) demand very high and theoretically 'voluntary' parental contributions, which, if tested at law, might prove technically illegal. The government prefer to describe their policies in terms of more competition and greater institutional 'independence'; and the most malign side effect of this competitive independence is a malign 'atomisation' of each school and each pupil within it. The fetish of educational competition has gone too far. Though all schools develop, by their nature, a natural culture of competition, the teacher's job is often to blunt this phenomenon when it becomes unpleasant and counterproductive.

The independence is illusory because it involves transferring schools from the gentle frying pan of local supervision into the bureaucratic fire of national regulation with competition as its overriding criterion. The function of the government's two powerful quango regulators, QCA and OFSTED – the first controlling the nature of assessment and the second publicising its outcomes – has been to entrench league table competition and make creative cooperation between pupils and between institutions more difficult. A possibility of change, however, is appearing on the horizon in the shape of a third and unlikely regulator – the Charities Commission.

A Draft Charities Bill, which has been discussed at length in committee, but will only be introduced after the general election, contains fundamental reforms to charity law; its passage through parliament will be difficult because it will ask awkward questions about why fee-paying schools are charities and force them to find a much more exacting definition of their purposes. Hitherto, if you run a school and do not seek to make a profit out of it, unless entry is absurdly restricted, you get charitable status simply because you are providing education. Soon the presumption that the provision of education is automatically charitable will disappear; all independent fee-paying schools (and indeed fee paying hospitals) will have to prove to the Charities Commission that their activities bring 'public benefit'.

'Public benefit' has, since the Statute of Elizabeth introduced charity law 400 years ago, been a difficult concept to pin down; the courts, well over a century ago, invented the phrase as an extra criterion for charitable status, on top of education, religion and the relief of poverty, to encourage 19th century voluntary activity. The current government has made it clear that it has no intention of defining the phrase in law, though it has not ruled out offering informal advice about its meaning. In defending this refusal to be specific, Fiona Mactaggart, the Home Office minister in charge of the draft bill, said that the government could not 'find criteria which could be equally applied to a village hall, to the Anti-Vivisection

Society [or] to Eton'. There was, however, for obvious political reasons, an understandable reluctance to set out its precise policy on the public/private divide in education because some of No 10's third way philosophers are in denial about the very existence of this phenomenon and the prime minister prefers privatisation by stealth.

Others, however are not in denial and have begun to put forward concrete proposals for a win/win policy – narrowing the divide and improving education for all – especially in our cities. One of Britain most distinguished educational administrators, Tim Brighouse, has analysed the pecking order of different grades of comprehensive school which have developed in our cities over past decades and concluded that a more effective structure of secondary education would be one in which a cooperative and collegiate culture began to replace one of competitive, atomized institutions.

Brighouse has proposed a two tier formal arrangement in which all secondary schools, public and private, share resources. He describes it as an 'an ideal where all young people, whatever their 'home-base' school, whether in the state or private sector, take substantial periods of their education together.. within a collegiate framework which acknowledges that secondary education involves belonging to at least two institutions - the school and the 'collegiate' to which it is attached.'

When the task of finding criteria for public benefit and imposing them on independent schools is passed to the Charities Commission, their task will not be an easy one. Some have suggested purely financial criteria – based on the magnitude of the fees and the tax exemption benefits enjoyed. But the Commission has always had a far wider remit than the regulation of charitable cash; and common sense dictates that its new powers over the definition of public benefit should include a much broader 'social equity' remit for the Charities Commission to develop – as they have in other areas of their work. Eton, like other public schools, was founded as a charity for 12 poor scholars in the parish of Eton, competent in Donatus (the standard Latin grammar textbook of the day) and plainsong. A high master of Winchester College confirmed to a Commons select committee 30 years ago that the reason the public schools were colonised by the rich and then confirmed by the courts as still charitable was because of the Catch 22 reality that too few poor children were mastering Latin grammar.

The next phase of the public schools' existence - their division into charitable sheep and uncharitable goats - will be a very slow burn process. The Bill will not become law until the autumn of 2006 at the earliest and years of litigation will follow. But some independent schools, aware of the future, are already jumping the gun, with initial inventive ideas - like lending playing fields to local comprehensives. Previous attempts to resolve the issue through committees of the 'great and good' - the Fleming Committee in 1944 and of the Public Schools Commission (1968, 1970) were brushed away easily by fee paying schools.

But the draft bill's 'public benefit' formula is a different matter since it seeks to put all charities on the same footing. Nor is it new. In 1974 a Commons select committee, of which I was a member and drafter of the wording, recommended a test of 'public benefit' as the overriding consideration with that of education. Though the idea did not appeal to the Callaghan government, it survived over the years in Labour party manifestos and has now resurfaced.

So here, prime minister, you are faced with an historic 'modernising' opportunity - to follow up the aspiration of one of your predecessors, John Major, to blunt the growth of the class divide in Britain. The refusal of any government to define 'public benefit' could be an advantage to you. If you and your education minister make the right sort of noises commending a co-operative vision of the charitable duties of these schools, the Charities Commission and the courts could well follow your lead, especially, now that nearly 20% of the 16 -18 year old secondary school cohort is in independent schools; and you could give the other education regulators, OFSTED and QCA, alongside the Charity Commission, a general 'equity' remit, to encourage institutional Cupertino.

The idea of voluntary public/private Cupertino could well be tempting for fee paying schools not only as a charitable status preservative but also as an escape from the league table culture many heartily dislike. Membership of a co-operative, collegiate and inclusive mix of state and independent schools could open up all sorts of new opportunities for pupils in smaller, less generously resourced schools. It also envisages the eventual emergence of voluntary initiatives with four or five to even perhaps a dozen secondary schools working more closely together in our cities. The idea would interest the Teacher Training Agency with its new responsibility of putting professional development days to better use; it could be relatively unbureaucratic; and may even be welcomed by some LEAs as a bulwark between ministerial diktat and individual schools.

The proposals could be the beginning of a new pattern in which the public and private sectors cooperate and learn from each other - especially how to avoid the twin evils of unnecessary bureaucracy and unnecessary competition. Brighouse's proposals are based on the need to look at ten facets of secondary education: learning; teaching; curriculum; assessment; quality of staff, internal organisational arrangements of the school, particularly the timetable; the (hidden) curriculum beyond the school; the context of the school and its pupils and their origins; the relationship of the school with other schools and other institutions; and the purpose of secondary education and schooling itself; and to understand that voluntary coordination over these facets, within an environment wider than the individual school, could massively improve educational standards.

As he puts it: 'They are all interrelated cogs. Move one and you affect another.' It is altogether possible that a this wider collegiate structure – especially in our cities – and a wider educational remit for the three school regulators – OFSTED, QCA and the Charities Commission – could prove a new comprehensive vision for an inclusive 21st century learning environment.

Chris Price is former Vice Chancellor of Leeds Metropolitan University and Chair of the House of Commons Education Select Committee